After **GOD'S** *Heart*

After **GOD'S** *Heart*

A Study in **BROKENNESS**
From the Life of David

ELIZABETH VIERA TALBOT

Pacific Press®
Publishing Association

Nampa, Idaho | Oshawa, Ontario, Canada
www.pacificpress.com

Cover design by Gerald Lee Monks
Cover art by arrangement with © Greg Olsen
Outside editor: Aivars Ozolins, PhD

The author assumes full responsibility for the accuracy of all facts and quotations as cited in this book.

Additional copies of this book are available by calling toll-free 1-800-765-6955 or by visiting http://www.adventistbookcenter.com.

Unless otherwise noted, Scripture quotations are taken from the NEW AMERICAN STANDARD BIBLE®, Copyright © 1960, 1962, 1963, 1968, 1971, 1972, 1973, 1975, 1977, 1995 by The Lockman Foundation. Used by permission. www.lockman.org.

Scriptures quoted from CEV are from Contemporary English Version®. Copyright © 1995 American Bible Society. All rights reserved.

Scripture marked *The Message* is taken from *The Message*. Copyright © 1993, 1994, 1995, 1996, 2000, 2001, 2002. Used by permission of NavPress Publishing Group.

Scripture quotations marked NIV® are from THE HOLY BIBLE, NEW INTERNATIONAL VERSION®. Copyright © 1973, 1978, 1984, 2011 by Biblica, Inc.® Used by permission. All rights reserved worldwide.

Scripture marked NKJV is taken from the New King James Version®. Copyright © 1982 by Thomas Nelson. Used by permission. All rights reserved.

ISBN: 978-0-8163-6330-8

August 2017

edication

This book is lovingly dedicated to my father, Dr. Juan Carlos Viera, who rests in Jesus until that glorious day when the Savior will call him from death to eternal life. He was a man after God's own heart, whose words and example inspired and motivated me to believe and to serve my Master.

And to Jesus, my Savior, Redeemer, and King, who considered me worth leaving the heavenly realms and dying here on earth. His love is so great and so high for broken people like me that I could never fully comprehend it. His grace will eternally amaze me

$\mathcal{T}$able of Contents

CHAPTER 1

*A*nointed

He had virtually no voice left, yet he managed to somehow whisper, word by word, the entire Psalm 23. His brilliant mind was still intact even though his strength had left him. This was the last section of Scripture I heard from my dad's lips as he lay on his deathbed, waiting for the inevitable, in full surrender and without fear. "Even though I walk through the valley of the shadow of death, I will fear no evil, for You are with me . . ." Valley of death—with *no* fear—how is that possible? The answer follows in the same verse: "for *You* are with me." I will never forget the experience of watching my dad face the surety of death in full assurance of faith, completely certain of the ending: "And I will dwell in the house of the LORD *forever*" (verses 4, 6; emphasis added).

My father was a man who taught me, by words and actions, about the heart of God and what it meant to trust in Him. In fact, both of my parents fully trusted and rested in the arms of their heavenly Shepherd—in life and in death, in sickness and in health, in difficulties and in abundance. My father trusted his Shepherd even during his struggle with three different types of cancer that afflicted him over a period of fifteen years in spite of his healthy lifestyle. That is why my homily at his memorial service, based on Psalm 23, was entitled "Rest Assured." I admire my dad very much and for many reasons, not the least of which is that his peaceful demeanor welled out of the spring of his Jesus-centered faith, even to his last breath. He was the same person in public and in private—his God-induced integrity inspires me and will continue to do so for eternity. Throughout his life, he possessed a serenity that I desire for myself, a tranquil fortitude grounded in his conviction that Jesus died for him, and that his past, present, and future rested in the arms of his Creator-Redeemer. And even though my father was a religious leader, a minister, and a shepherd of his flock, he was primarily a sheep following the Good Shepherd, who had laid down His life for him. Jesus said, "My sheep know my voice" (John 10:27, CEV).

All of us yearn for such an intimacy with God.

I am certain that my parents will recognize their Shepherd's voice in the resurrection morning and will follow Him throughout eternity.

What is it about Psalm 23 and its writer that ministers to us, regardless of our upbringing, race, age, or situation? Whether we live in abundance—in green pastures and waters of rest—or find ourselves in the valley of the shadow of death, we all can relate to the song of this sling-hurling ancient shepherd boy who cried a lot and who could sing and play his lyre to soothe even a mad king—and who later became a king himself. David, the only person in the Bible called a man after God's own heart, inspires me with his vulnerability and his yearning for intimacy with God—when he was in the pit of sin and when he was on the top of the world. And he discovered that the only path to a deep soul-searching awareness of God's love for us leads through brokenness. When we are broken, we have nothing to use as payment. And that's when we can fully accept God's gift of grace, salvation, and purpose. All is a gift. And we are filled with praise and thanksgiving, even while in the cave of affliction and pain. Yes! All of us yearn for such an intimacy with God. And hopefully through this book we will get to know a bit more about David, the man after God's heart, who also foreshadowed the Davidic King who would later come to lay down His life for His sheep. I can't wait to explore how a man like David, with so many ups and downs, who committed grave sins, who pretended to be crazy, and who was conscience-stricken for cutting off a corner of the robe of a maniac-king, was viewed by God as a man "after My heart" (Acts 13:22). Thanks for joining me in this exciting biblical journey! Let's dive into the Scriptures! Here we go! Woo-hoo!

God's plan

As the prophet Samuel grieved over the failings of the king whose heart had departed from God, he received a heavenly message to go to Bethlehem to anoint a new king. Interestingly enough, the crazy king, Saul himself, had already received this verdict from God through Samuel: "Your kingdom shall not endure. The LORD has sought out for Himself a *man after His own heart*, and the LORD has appointed him as ruler over His people" (1 Samuel 13:14; emphasis added). What kind of regal, majestic king was this that God had prepared for Himself? Oh boy, was Samuel in for a surprise!

"Now the LORD said to Samuel, 'How long will you grieve over Saul, since I have rejected him from being king over Israel? Fill your horn with oil and go; I will send you to Jesse the Bethlehemite, for I have selected a king for Myself among his sons' " (1 Samuel 16:1). Since the prophet, aware of the increasing madness of the king, is afraid for his life, the Lord sends him to Bethlehem to sacrifice a heifer (verse 2). So Samuel heads to Bethlehem with an animal in tow and a horn of oil hidden from prying eyes, in order to anoint a new king.

When everything around me seems to fall apart, I need to remember that God has a plan.

God had a plan. I love it! When everything around me

seems to fall apart, I need to remember that God has a plan. Nothing takes Him by surprise; He is never early or late; nothing escapes His notice or is above His head. He has a plan and possesses the power to execute it! That's good news, isn't it? He usually doesn't reveal His whole plan to us, though; only the next step we need to take. But He knows the full plan, and we can trust Him with it. Back in Bethlehem, the scope of His plan was greater than anyone could have imagined! One thousand years later, in the same fields where Samuel found the future shepherd-king, a choir of angels would announce the birth of the Savior of the world, the King of heaven and earth, the descendant of David who would set us free from sin. Same town, same fields, same plan. God always acted in patterns, geographically and historically, so that we wouldn't miss the Savior when He came. *He was The Plan* all along!

And God said to Samuel: "I will show you what you shall do" (verse 3). Great! Hurry up! Let's get going. Imagine how exciting it is to anoint a new king! So what exactly was God looking for in this new ruler, the man after His own heart?

God's view
The elders of Bethlehem are a little nervous to see such a great religious figure in their seemingly unimportant little town. But Samuel sets their minds at ease by explaining

that he has come to sacrifice. He also consecrates Jesse and his sons and invites them to the sacrifice (verses 4, 5). All is going as planned. Surely this prophet of God will spot the new king immediately. He has an eye for these things. After all, he's done it before. And let's remember that Saul was tall, a head above everyone else in Israel! This new king wouldn't be less, for sure. Right? *Wrong!*

God always acted in patterns, geographically and historically, so that we wouldn't miss the Savior when He came.

Have you experienced that—when you think you know what God wants, when you know the way, God throws you a curveball? I am so glad that even God's prophets are human! Because that's exactly what happened to Samuel. When Jesse's sons entered and Samuel saw Eliab, he thought: "Surely the LORD's anointed is before Him" (verse 6). But God made this a teaching moment for him. The Lord responded with one of the most important aphorisms we have in the Bible regarding God's view of humanity: "But the LORD said to Samuel, 'Do not look at his appearance or at the height of his stature, because I have rejected him; for God sees not as man sees, for man looks at the outward appearance, but the LORD looks at the heart' " (verse 7). Yikes!

Yep! So true! We often get stuck in externals, pomp

and circumstance. The parade continued, and all the sons of Jesse seemed more than qualified. Eliab, Abinadab, Shammah—all seven boys. But God had not chosen any of them (verses 6–10). Had Samuel gotten the wrong town? A different address? Was the GPS broken? But the prophet was a quick learner, and he asked Jesse: " 'Are these all the children?' And he said, 'There remains yet the youngest, and behold, he is tending the sheep.' Then Samuel said to Jesse, 'Send and bring him; for we will not sit down until he comes here' " (verse 11). The youngest, a shepherd, had not even been invited to participate in the sacrifice with the rest of the family. By their standards he didn't qualify. The youngest wasn't their choice. But he was God's.

God's choice

I love it! I love it! I love this pattern of God: He chooses the reject, the underdog, the little one, the least, and the last. It makes me feel loved and accepted, with all my imperfections. God is in the business of choosing the unlikely ones. Woo-hoo!

There had been occasions when God had chosen the youngest sibling instead of the oldest (see Genesis 25:23; 48:14, 19–20)—but not for a king! Was it possible that He was choosing the youngest brother, a shepherd boy, as the king of Israel? "So he sent and brought him in. Now he was ruddy, with beautiful eyes and a handsome appearance. And the LORD said, 'Arise, anoint him; for this is he.' Then Samuel took the horn of oil and anointed him in the midst of his brothers; and the Spirit of the LORD came mightily upon David from that day forward" (verses 12, 13). David! This is the first time we encounter the name of this boy who would be king. No other person in the Bible bears that name. Only him, the man after God's own heart. And this is the first time that David meets Samuel. Later we are told of one other time the two of them met (1 Samuel 19:18).

He is given the Spirit of the Lord and enrolled in God's school of brokenness, where he is to learn things not taught in any other school.

So, Samuel anointed the unlikely candidate—the first of three times that David was anointed. The second was many years later when he was anointed as king over the house of Judah (see 2 Samuel 2:4), and the third, when he became the king over all Israel (see 2 Samuel 5:3). But all of this is still far in the future. For the present time, in Bethlehem, he is given the Spirit of the Lord (1 Samuel 16:13) and enrolled in God's school of brokenness, where he is to learn things not taught in any other school. His soul will be trained to seek after God's heart. Just like you and me, he must be trained in the art of not returning the spears that are thrown at him. He must learn to sing and cry and to never stop talking to God no matter how dark it gets. He must be trained to pray and sing in the pits of despair, in caves of abandonment, and in mountain strongholds, addressing God as "*my* God." The shepherd boy will learn to depend on God as his own Shepherd. When his heart is broken, he will find comfort in the only One who can restore the soul.

David has been anointed the king to unify the nation, to place Israel on the map, to be part of God's covenant line, and to be included in the lineage of the coming Davidic Messianic King, the Savior of the world and the eternal King. Oh! And did I mention it? He has been anointed to be a man after God's own heart; therefore, he will attend God's school for the brokenhearted.

> The LORD is my shepherd,
> I shall not want.
> He makes me lie down in green pastures;
> He leads me beside quiet waters.
> *He restores my soul* (Psalm 23:1–3;
>   emphasis added).

Individual or Small Group Study Questions

1. Do you feel connected to the story of David in the Bible? Why?

2. Why does God in the Bible seem to always choose the least, the last, the most insignificant, and so forth?

3. Explain the meaning of 2 Corinthians 12:9. What is the relationship between grace and weakness?

4. Samuel thought he would recognize the new king by his appearance. Do you think we often judge people by appearances? How can we switch to God's method instead?

5. Why was David, with his checkered track record, a man after God's own heart?

CHAPTER 2

Chosen

Giants are scary—even if they are only a product of your own imagination. I remember my first experience with a giant. I was a little girl, and my mom and I had gone out for a ride. Part of her job was collecting a payment from a company, and she told me to stay inside the locked car for just a few minutes. At that time, it was OK to leave a child in the car for a short period. It was a safe area, and she would return shortly. The window was partway open, and I dutifully sat, reading my children's magazines. However, I had heard of a mysterious and unusual people who lived in that town. They looked and dressed differently, and I had decided in my young mind that they were to be feared. With that in the back of my mind I was a little bit on the lookout just to make sure I wasn't kidnapped or in peril.

Giants are scary—even if they are only a product of your own imagination.

Shortly after my mother was out of sight, a girl my age, clearly belonging to the "suspect" group, approached our car. Unexpectedly, she demanded that I give her my magazines, which I refused. She then responded in a most terrifying way: "I will call my mom—you'll see what she will do!" And here's where my imagination kicked into high gear. In my mind I saw a giant woman coming to the car, forcing the door open, and taking me away to never ever see my loved ones again. The fact that it was just my imagination did not make it less real for me! I couldn't fight this giant—I was just a child! What should I do? I felt utterly desperate. The adrenaline rush helped me squeeze through the small opening in the window. I left the car crying at the top of my lungs. I thought my life was in danger, and anything seemed better than staying in the car! I didn't know exactly where my mother was. I started walking down the street, crying so loudly that my mother heard me and came running out to see what was going on. Between sobs, I tried to describe to her the object of my imagination: a giant woman, ready to take me away forever! Naturally we never saw the "giant" woman, but she was definitely real to me! My mother was never able to figure out how I could slide through that small opening in the window. Desperate times call for desperate measures—and giants qualify as desperate times.

A desperate army

The battle was going to be important, as we can surmise from the details in 1 Samuel 17. The first verse starts by stating: "Now the Philistines gathered their armies for battle" (verse 1). These powerful and highly civilized people, the people of the sea living before 1000 B.C., were trained and seasoned warriors. The valley of Elah (verse 2) was of utmost importance for them because it was the primary point of entry into the hill country. It was about twelve miles west of Bethlehem. After three verses of geographical details, we meet the giant: "Then a champion came out from the armies of the Philistines named Goliath, from Gath, whose height was six cubits and a span" (verse 4). The giant's name, Goliath, is only used twice: in verse 4 and verse 23; all of the other times he will be referred to as "the Philistine" (twenty-seven times in this story). He is tall—really tall! About three meters tall. And he is the representative of the Philistine army.

As if his stature wasn't scary enough, the next three verses (verses 5–7) detail his intimidating armor and weapons, shielding every inch of his body (except part of his face). Verses 5 through 7 make it clear that it is humanly impossible to prevail against such an overwhelming champion. And it is not only the giant (verse 4) or his weapons (verses 5–7) that are intimidating. Even his words (verses 8–11) are making everyone run for cover: "I defy the ranks of Israel this day; give me a man that we may fight together" (verse 10). Even Israel's own giant, King Saul, who is a head taller than everyone else in Israel, is now terrified: "When Saul and all Israel heard these words of the Philistine, they were dismayed and greatly afraid" (verse 11; see also verse 24). Yes, to put it mildly,

> *God calls everyone to live for His glory and to expand His kingdom.*

this army is desperate! They all want to flee the scene! And the giant taunts the armies of the Living God for forty days (verse 16). Interestingly, forty days is a period of testing in the Bible, to encourage trust in God (the Flood, the spies in Canaan, Jonah's message to Nineveh, Jesus' temptations in the desert, etc.). Everyone is desperate and looking for a solution, but there is none. Who would have thought that God had prepared a boy after His own heart for such a time as this?

Who is this?

One of the things that always gets me about David is his humble and ordinary beginnings. The three older brothers who had been introduced to Samuel (1 Samuel 16:6–9), are now in Saul's army (1 Samuel 17:13). David, probably too young to fight, kept alternating between Saul and his father's flock in Bethlehem (verse 15). David was serving Saul in the court, often playing and singing as seen in the subsequent chapters, but for some reason Saul didn't recognize him in this story (verses 55–58). Don't you love how God uses ordinary people for His glory? I am so thankful for that! God calls shepherds and carpenters, homemakers and gardeners, moms, dads, kids, business people, doctors, and lawyers. He calls everyone to live for His glory and to expand His kingdom.

Jesse sends David with supplies to his brothers on the battlefield. When David arrives, he hears the words of the Philistine champion and indignantly inquires: "*Who is this* uncircumcised Philistine, that he should taunt the armies of the living God?" (verse 26; emphasis added). He is not annoyed for himself but passionate for God. I had to learn to choose my battles carefully. When I joined the ministry, I realized right away that I needed God's wisdom in this area—and fast! I learned to choose only those battles that pertain to God's name and the integrity of the gospel message. I understood that we don't need to defend ourselves every time someone attacks us personally. But when the gospel is on the line, God places a fire in our bellies to proclaim the good news clearly, no matter the consequences.

As David arrived at the battlefield, the giant was shouting insults, defying Israel and their God. The timing of these events tells us that God was acting behind the scenes, training His *chosen one* to trust in Him even in the most impossible situations. David would become a core character in the covenantal plan of redemption, and just like us, he had to learn that it is not about us but about God and His ability to save. He was becoming a man after God's heart—experiencing his own *powerlessness* and God's *powerfulness*!

Some people overheard David and took him to King Saul, where he made his intent clear: "Your servant will go and fight with this Philistine" (verse 32). Saul replied: "You are not able . . . ; you are but a youth while he has been a warrior from his youth" (verse 33). You are a young kid, but he is an experienced fighter! And his armor! And his weapons! And his size! No way you can win this one!

The Lord will deliver me!

If you are to fulfill God's purpose for your life, you will need to learn to discern His voice from all the others. David had to lend a deaf ear to Saul's voice (verse 33), his brother's voice (verse 28), and probably the voice in his own head that kept stating the obvious: you are too small, too young, too inexperienced, blah, blah, blah. Instead he decided to focus on God; not on the giant, not on himself, not on the others. David encouraged his soul, and King Saul, by remembering how in the past the Lord had delivered the lion and the bear into his hands (verse 37). Goliath would be no different: "The LORD who delivered me from the paw of the lion and from the paw of the bear, He will deliver me from the hand of this Philistine" (verse 37).

David would face the giant in the name of the LORD of hosts!

Finally, Saul agreed and tried to clothe David in his armor, which was a bad idea. We are all different, and God never intended for us to try to be someone else or to wear someone else's "armor." It didn't work, and David "took them off" (verse 39).

Then David headed to a dry riverbed in the valley of Elah and picked up five smooth stones (verse 40). I had the privilege of standing in that dried brook, and I also picked up stones. It was quite an emotional experience for me, standing right there, in the middle of the valley, with the two hills overlooking the very place where David and Goliath faced each other. Once again, I was reminded of how God has the ability to take something as ordinary as a smooth stone and use it to win an extraordinary battle. David placed the stones in his shepherd's bag (verse 40) and with the sling in his hand approached the giant.

David was quite busy right before the face-off (verses 39, 40): he girded, tried, removed, took, chose, put, and approached. But it wasn't his excitement, his energy, or his ability that won the battle. No! He would face the giant in the name of the LORD of hosts!

"The battle is the LORD's"!

The following fourteen verses narrate the actual duel between Goliath and David and its aftermath (verses 41–54). When the giant saw David, he cursed him by his gods (verse 43) and promised to give his flesh to the birds and beasts for food (verse 44). David didn't blink but gave his longest speech in this chapter: "You come to me with a sword, a spear, and a javelin, but I come to you in the *name of the LORD of hosts* [*Yahweh seba'ot*], the God of the armies of Israel, whom you have taunted. This day the LORD will deliver you up into my hands, and I will strike you down and remove your head from you. And I will give the dead bodies of the army of the Philistines this day to the birds of the sky and the wild beasts of the earth, that all the earth may know that there is a God in Israel, and that all this assembly may know that the LORD does not deliver by sword or spear, for the battle is the LORD's and He will give you into our hands" (verses 45–47; emphasis added). Woo-hoo! You go, David!

The powerful name of God "LORD of hosts" is used 241 times in the Jewish Scriptures. Amazing! This is not one of many gods, like the Philistine claimed. No! This is *the* God of the armies of heaven and earth! And it is *His name* that is on the line. David's passion is for God's reputation. And then he says something that I need to remember every day: "*the battle is the LORD's*"! Not mine, not yours . . . but God's! And God's ways are different from our ways. The Philistines had the tallest champion, the most powerful weapons, and the best training. But God just needed a man after His own heart. And He chose David.

Chosen

The Representative

It was quite common in that culture to go into battle through a *representative*. But it is even more important for us to understand that principle in the spiritual and theological realm. You see, this is the reason we can live with the assurance of salvation: because our Representative, Jesus, has fought and won on our behalf. Adam, the representative of the human race, chose to disobey God, and we all became sinful and mortal. Jesus, the Second Adam, through His obedience to the point of death on the cross, won for everyone who chooses Him as Representative. "So then as through one transgression there resulted condemnation to all men, even so through one act of righteousness there resulted justification of life to all men. For as through the one man's disobedience the many were made sinners, even so through the obedience of the One the many will be made righteous" (Romans 5:18, 19). This is the good news of the gospel of Jesus Christ: we have eternal salvation, not because *we* are powerful and able soldiers in the

> This is the good news of the gospel of Jesus Christ: we have eternal salvation, not because *we* are powerful and able soldiers in the battle between good and evil, but because Jesus fought in our place and won. Woo-hoo!

battle between good and evil, but because Jesus fought in our place and won. Woo-hoo!

Now, back to David. He fought as a representative of all Israel, in the name and power of the God of Israel. When David was done with his discourse (1 Samuel 17:45–47), instead of running away like everyone else had during the past forty days, "David ran quickly *toward* the battle line to meet the Philistine" (verse 48; emphasis added)—and the rest is history. How is that for a passion and purpose! I love it! *God* gave David the victory! And this is the David we all admire: triumphant, passionate, victorious, assured, ready, willing, and able. And yet this is just the beginning of David's story. Everyone cheers for the strong and the powerful, and yet God's power is made perfect in our weakness (2 Corinthians 12:9). And David had to learn that truth when he faced some of the greater giants in his life: doubt, fear, loneliness, unfairness, persecution, jealousy, and his own sin and pride. Those are the types of giants that are defeated by God when He enrolls us in the school of brokenness.

Individual or Small Group Study Questions

1. What was the main different between David and everyone else in Israel when facing the giant? Why is it that sometimes we focus more on the size of our giants and not so much on how big our God is?
2. Why is it important to remember how God has delivered us from difficulties in the past?
3. Do you sometimes try to fit in someone else's armor?
4. How is Jesus our "Representative" who took our place in the battle and why does this give us assurance for the future?
5. What are the theological and practical life implications of believing that "the battle is the Lord's"?

CHAPTER 3

*M*istreated

Unexpected adverse seasons are difficult. And typically these storms bring unpredictable timing and a lot of change combined with a mixture of pain and fear—and we don't know what to do next or how to keep our faith alive. Maybe you were served divorce papers, or perhaps you lost your job. Or perhaps you've just received bad news from your doctor. Suddenly everything changes. Now what?

I was young and ready to experience life when I decided to try a new venture by starting a computer company dealing with an integrated industry-specific software. We leased our office space, hired employees, and launched the business. However, we found out very soon that the competition was very fierce. Since we didn't have enough funds to hire a marketing person, I had to go out to do sales, even though I hated it. One day I was sitting on the floor of the office and tried to get up but couldn't. I had a sharp pain in my knee; something was terribly wrong. At the hospital I was told that my meniscus had been crushed and I needed an immediate surgery. *What? I can't do that! I don't have time! I have to take care of my company and make enough money to pay my employees! How long would recovery take? Why can't this happen next year, when we are established?* But usually we don't get to choose the timing of a storm.

And just like that, the tide changed. They tried to do arthroscopic surgery, but it didn't work. So they had to cut open my knee (a big cut, by the way!), and I was unable to walk for about two months. Looking back, I realize that during that time of waiting God was training me to trust Him with my daily tasks, my future, my anxieties, my bills, and everything else. These unexpected events brought some really difficult financial and emotional changes. But God was using this time to teach me something that would become handy later on when I had to face even more overwhelming circumstances. Eventually I had to close this company just as I had to close other important chapters in my life. But little by little God was teaching me a simple but profound lesson: *Trust Me!* Why is it that we learn certain lessons *only* in the school of brokenness? I sometimes wonder . . .

Change of plans

Saul, the king who was getting crazier by the minute, was having spiritual issues, to say the least. David would play the harp in Saul's court so that when the evil spirit came upon the king, the music would help him (see 1 Samuel 16:18–23). When David killed Goliath, Saul realized that he could do a lot more than play the harp, so he did not want David to go home anymore (1 Samuel 18:2). "David went out wherever Saul sent him, and prospered; and Saul set him over the men of war" (verse 5). That was a brilliant plan! The victorious David would now help the king to battle his enemies. Surely this shepherd boy turned warrior will bring victory because the Spirit of God is with him! Awesome! That's how we like it!

It is important to remember that there are storms that come with no wrongdoing on our part.

But suddenly the plans change. The narrative takes us behind the scenes to reveal the relational problems besetting the king's heart. As Saul and David returned from the battle with the Philistines, the women came out to greet them with instruments, singing, and great joy (verse 6). The women sang "Saul has slain his thousands, and David his ten thousands" (verse 7). And that was it—that was all it took to throw this insecure king and his ego for a loop. Saul became angry and from that day on was always *suspicious* of David (verses 8, 9). Crazy! Isn't it? A simple song, with a nice and common rhyme, suddenly created the perfect storm in Saul's heart. It is important to remember that there are storms that come with no wrongdoing on our part. We live in a sinful world where good people die from cancer, kids get killed by drunk drivers, and hillsides collapse on the homes of innocent families. I praise the Lord for His promises to be with us always (Matthew 28:20) and that one day He will put an end to all the pain, sickness, and death (Revelation 21:4)!

Back to our story. At the king's court everything seemed normal. David played his harp, and then all of a sudden, "Saul hurled the spear for he thought, 'I will pin David to the wall.' But David escaped from his presence twice" (1 Samuel 18:11). Excuse me! Did we miss something? What happened? Saul tried to kill David? (By the way, this wouldn't be the last time! See 1 Samuel 19:9, 10). What about Saul's plans? Well . . . plans change.

Downward spiral

Unbelievably, Saul was afraid of David because the Lord was with him and everyone in Judah and Israel loved him (1 Samuel 18:12–16). Saul didn't just mistreat David; he wanted him dead. So the king came up with some more *subtle* ways of getting rid of David. Saul's daughter Michal loved David, and the king saw an opportunity to fulfill his evil designs through her: "I will give her to him that she may become a *snare* to him, and that the hand of the Philistines may be against him" (verse 21; emphasis added). The jealousy monster has no limits. Saul hated David so much that he was willing to use his own daughter as a bait. Furthermore, he was hoping that David would die trying to supply the outrageous "dowry" the king demanded: "Saul then said, 'Thus you shall say to David, "The king does not desire any dowry except a hundred foreskins of the Philistines, to take vengeance on the king's enemies." ' *Now Saul planned to make David fall by the hand of the Philistines*" (verse 25; emphasis added). David struck down, not one hundred but, two hundred Philistine men. Saul's subtle ways were not working, so he switched to an open and overt campaign to kill David.

> *When we become negligent in heeding God's voice speaking to our heart, usually the downward spiral is quick.*

"Now Saul told Jonathan his son and all his servants to put David to death" (1 Samuel 19:1). This is the first time Saul publicly announced his plan to exterminate the man after God's heart. When we become negligent in heeding God's voice speaking to our heart, usually the downward spiral is quick. Now, for no apparent reason at all, Saul is openly hunting down the one in whom the Spirit of the Lord is obviously found. Such a season in our lives is very troubling. We don't know why bad things are happening. David obviously could have thrown the spear back or laid a trap for Saul or used his sling. But David respected Saul as the king, appointed by God, and did not want to harm him. While Saul's methods and motives are spiraling down, out of control, David is being trained to choose different methods and trust in the Lord because he, too, would be king—and not a king like Saul. But things were definitely not what David had expected. Can you relate?

There is a book written by Gene Edwards, entitled *A Tale of Three Kings*, that has helped me immensely. In it, he discusses the need for David to be trained in the school of brokenness. Edwards points out that David would be king but not after the order of Saul. And the core proposition of his book is that *God used Saul to kill the Saul in David*, so that when David became the king he wouldn't be like Saul.[1] Isn't that deep? Whenever I find myself in unfair circumstances or feeling mistreated or oppressed in one way or another, I reread this book, and it reminds me that my brokenness can bring glory to God.

> *My brokenness can bring glory to God.*

"There is a time for every event under heaven" (Ecclesiastes 3:1–8), and in David's life, *a time to run* had arrived.

God with us

"The LORD was with him" (1 Samuel 18:12); "The LORD was with him" (verse 14); "The LORD was with David" (verse 28). Really? And if the Lord is with David, why does he have to run? Why escape? Why not confront, fight, battle, and throw spears? So glad you asked! Because if he fought and threw spears, he would be as crazy as King Saul . . . and God needed a man after His own heart, a different type of king. Amazing!

Jonathan, the king's son, became very close to David and protected him from his father's murderous plans (see 1 Samuel 19, 20). Even the king's daughter, David's wife, helped David escape after her father tried once again to "pin David to the wall" (1 Samuel 19:8–17). It is important to mention that, during these sudden storms of pain, God usually sends people to remind us that He is with us. God encourages us with godly advice and friendships, and sometimes He sends trustworthy listeners. God is amazing! I will be eternally grateful for the spiritual wisdom and encouragement of my close friends at the times when everything felt cold and dark around me.

While Saul's methods and motives are spiraling down, out of control, David is being trained to choose different methods and trust in the Lord.

I want to mention two other principles. When David escaped from his own house with the help of his wife, he fled to Ramah: "Now David fled and escaped and came to Samuel at Ramah, and told him all that Saul had done to him" (verse 18). I love this verse. David not only looked up to Samuel because he was a prophet but he was also reminded of his calling when he first met Samuel. This was the prophet of God who had anointed him king by divine command—the man who could remind him that he was the chosen one, the man after God's own heart. We can do the same: go to where we can be reminded of our calling.

The second place is Nob, where David went to see Ahimelech the priest (see 1 Samuel 21:1). And something amazing happened there! David received food: the bread of the Presence that had been removed. Some scholars see in this event a reminder for David that God's presence was with him. But the part that really gets me is what comes next. "David said to Ahimelech, 'Now is there not a spear or a sword on hand? For I brought neither my sword nor my weapons with me, because the king's matter was urgent.' Then the priest said, 'The sword of Goliath the Philistine, whom you killed in the valley of Elah, behold, it is wrapped in a cloth behind the ephod; if you would take it for yourself, take it. For there is no other except it here.' And David said, 'There is none like it; give it to me' " (verses 8, 9). Wow! How is that for a reminder? I can picture God smiling at the sight. The sword of Goliath! I believe with all my heart that God used this moment to remind David that with the power of the LORD of hosts on his side he would get through this. God is an expert in being triumphant in the midst of apparent impossibilities. This was the reminder of a *giant* victory to encourage the heart of this fugitive, who was enrolled in the school of brokenness to grow closer to God's heart.

> God is an expert in being triumphant in the midst of apparent impossibilities.

Perfected through suffering

Jesus, the descendant of David, also enrolled in the school of brokenness. The result of the pain He endured would be eternal life for many, and that was good enough for the Savior. "But we do see Him who was made for a little while lower than the angels, namely, Jesus, because of the suffering of death crowned with glory and honor, so that by the grace of God He might taste death for everyone. For it was fitting for Him, for whom are all things, and through whom are all things, in bringing many sons to glory, *to perfect the author of their salvation through sufferings*" (Hebrews 2:9, 10; emphasis added). Jesus was perfected as a Savior through sufferings. And I will thank Him for eternity, because He is the only reason why I am saved.

Mistreated

David, one thousand years before Christ, would become a man after God's own heart through suffering and pain. God sent him friends, mentors, and powerful reminders of His presence along the way as He still does to us. And David, just like us, cried and sang his way into the next season: *caves*!

Individual or Small Group Study Questions

1. In the Bible we see people whom God uses in a special way to fulfill his purposes go through the school of brokenness. Is this necessary for us as well?
2. Why are sudden and unexpected life storms so scary? Feel free to share an example.
3. What would have been wrong if David had thrown the spear back in order to defend himself? Were his actions a sign of weakness or strength?
4. David had been anointed to be the king. Why did God allow so many bad things to happen in his life?
5. Why was suffering necessary for the Author of our salvation? (See Heb 2:9, 10).

---

1. Gene Edwards, *A Tale of Three Kings* (Wheaton, IL: Tyndale House Publishers, 1992).

$\mathscr{P}$ersecuted

I still remember the phone call even though it happened many years ago. My dad called me and asked if I could visit because my mom was having a very difficult day. You see, my mother and my father both went through really hard times with three different types of cancer each. Over the years they took turns caring for each other through chemo, radiation, and other tough times. Now it was my mother's turn to be bedridden. After a most difficult season of surgery, radiation, and chemo, it was very hard for her to see any light at the end of the dark tunnel. I must tell you that my mother was the most positive person that I have ever known. Even when losing her hair with chemo or when the tumors in her lungs were breaking her ribs, God enabled her to keep smiling, joking, trusting, and encouraging the people around her. So, this phone call asking for help was out of the ordinary.

When I arrived, I decided to put to use some of the skills I picked up in the art therapy classes that I took during my master's program in organizational behavior. We got colored pencils and paper, and I invited my mom to draw anything that came to her mind, starting from where she was now, then where she would be in the near future, and how she envisioned the future after that. With her very developed artistic side, she drew a dark hole to start and drew herself in it. Then she depicted herself climbing out of the hole and picking up flowers, then walking on a beautiful path filled with flowers and trees. The colors that she was using were getting brighter and the scenery happier and happier. Then on the right-hand side of the page, she colored the Pyramids, and I knew that her spirit was in the right place and that she would be all right. The reason why I was certain was that we were planning a trip to Egypt when all of this would be over, and I was so pleased to witness that she could envision herself traveling there. And we did! We went to Egypt and to many other places in the seven years that followed. I cherish a photo where she and I are riding camels and her hand is lifted up as if saying, "I made it!" She knew all along that God was with her, even in her darkest hours and the most difficult times.

The reason "in-between" times are so difficult is that we have no idea what point B looks like.

When I was going through my own dark "in-between" time (in-between: when you have left point A but don't know what point B will be), I learned a saying about faith: "Faith is not leaving point A to go to point B. It's just leaving point A." The reason "in-between" times are so difficult is that we have no idea what point B looks like. In his "in-between" period David will get closer and closer to God, writing some of the most heartrending psalms and sharing some of the most beautiful visualizations of God. And all of that happened when he had left point A in his life but had not yet arrived at point B—when he found himself in a real wilderness of the soul.

The wilderness of the soul

In just a few verses we learn that David is being persecuted and is dwelling in the hills, the forest, the wilderness, and the strongholds. Some of the many places mentioned are the cave of Adullam (1 Samuel 22:1), the forest of Hereth (verse 5), the wilderness of Ziph (1 Samuel 23:14), and the strongholds of Engedi (verse 29). David is not only dwelling in actual desolate places but has entered the *wilderness of the soul*, a place where we encounter God in a very personal and intimate way. It is a cocoon of the spiritual life.

> *David is not only dwelling in actual desolate places but has entered the wilderness of the soul, a place where we encounter God in a very personal and intimate way.*

Over the years, I have become passionately interested in the cocoon metaphor and the fact that the same place can be simultaneously a tomb and a womb, so to speak. The cocoon is the place where the caterpillar dies and the butterfly is born. And, this is where we find David.

It is during this dark time that David is being trained to be king, to lead people—some very *interesting* people, to say the least. "Everyone who was in distress, and everyone who was in debt, and everyone who was discontented gathered to him; and he became captain over them. Now there were about four hundred men with him" (1 Samuel 22:2). How would you like to start testing your leadership skills with such a group? He also learned the value of support, as his family gathered around him too (see verses 3, 4).

David learned to treat the undeserving current king with grace and compassion. While he and his men were hiding in a cave in Engedi, Saul, unaware of their presence, came into the same cave to relieve himself (you can read about this tense and yet somewhat amusing event in 1 Samuel 24:2–22). David's men thought this was a gift from God and strongly encouraged David to kill Saul, who had come with three thousand men to hunt down David. Instead, David cut off the edge of Saul's robe. Only a man after God's own heart could spare the life of a killer actively pursuing him. And yet a moment later David's conscience was bothering him. Why, you ask? Great question!

You see, at that time, cutting off the corner of someone's

robe signified breaking a covenant and terminating a relationship. In a divorce, the husband would cut off the corner of the wife's robe. Thus David, in fact, had sent a message to Saul that he no longer pledged allegiance to God's appointed king. Simply put, David had communicated that Saul's reign should be over and David's turn had come. The certainty of David's future as king was even acknowledged by Saul himself (see verses 20–22). But David was learning to wait for God to unfold His will and His timing—something that we usually learn during the wilderness of the soul. What we learn about God during this time will guide us during the rest of our lives. And we will learn to sing while in a cave.

During his time in the wilderness, David kept talking to God.

Songs and prayers of the heart

I had the privilege of visiting the desert of Engedi and the area where David hid in caves. It was an emotional experience to see the same hills, rocks, and caves that David saw. And perhaps for the first time I was able to truly relate to some of the most beautiful visualizations of God that David put in his songs and prayers. During his time in the wilderness, David kept talking to God, which is something that I have learned to do during the dark times in my adult years. Conversing with God during the bad times was a breakthrough for me. When I went through my own wilderness about twenty years ago, I attended some weekly groups for emotional and spiritual support. One day a minister who was struggling with his wife's reckless behavior shared a story that made the lightbulb go on in my mind.

The story was about a woman who for a very long time had been struggling with her husband's compulsive behaviors and yet had somehow managed to keep a happy appearance, hiding behind her smiles and a happy face. But one day her burden got too heavy: it was too much and too painful. Having just arrived home, still sitting in her car in the garage she started yelling at God at the top of her lungs, "How could you do this to me? Why did you allow this to happen?" Immediately she felt in her soul God talking to her and saying, "It's so nice to hear from you." I never forgot this story, because this was the time of darkness for me too, as I was learning my own songs and prayers of the heart. Being an emotionally strong person, it was easy for me to get into a place where I denied reality and always pretended to be OK— even when I wasn't. It was time for me to get real, and I knew that God wanted to hear from me, even though all I could muster in my prayer was: "Help!" "Why?" "Please!" or "Really?" By the way, have you noticed that some of the most desperate and heartfelt prayers consist of a single word?

During this "in-between" time, David wrote beautiful songs, or prayers, from his heart. Some of his psalms have at the beginning a description of the circumstances under which David wrote them. For example, the description found in Psalm 57 reads, "When he fled from Saul in the cave." And in Psalm 142, it reads "When he was in the cave. A Prayer." Please take a moment to read both psalms (57 and 142), and you will understand how David was feeling. I am particularly moved by phrases like "You are my refuge." David used the first person possessive pronoun, indicating that the Lord was not just *a* refuge, but "*my* refuge."

Standing in the wilderness of Engedi I could understand where David got some of his visualizations of God. This place is filled with rocks and strongholds like natural fortresses. For example, now when I read Psalm 144, I have a visualization in my soul: "Blessed be the LORD, my rock. . . . My lovingkindness and my fortress, my stronghold and my deliverer, my shield and He in whom I take refuge" (verses 1, 2). I started wondering what visualizations of God I may have that correspond to my needs and circumstances. What would you say to God? You are *my financial advisor*? Or You are *my best marriage therapist*? Or *my counselor*? I recently lost my father (my mother passed away two years earlier). For the first time I was an orphan. And now when I tell God, "You are *my Father*," these two words have a brand-new meaning . . . I am not an orphan. Now, why don't you try it? Fill in the blank:

"I cried out to You, O LORD; I said, 'You are *my*
_____' " (Psalm 142:5, paraphrase). When we find ourselves in a cave, God becomes real and personal, and we start an intimate and real relationship with our God and Savior. Perhaps you, too, will feel His voice saying, "It is so nice to hear from you!"

In-between

A few years ago my friend and fellow Bible student Alyssa Foll preached a sermon that I will never forget. It related to this cave time in the life of David, the "in-between"

His heart had to learn to beat in unison with God's heart, and that lesson was to be learned in the caves and strongholds of the wilderness.

time that she called "between anointing and appointing." It is the time period many of us are in, when we know that God has called us for a particular purpose, yet we find ourselves in a dark cave of adverse circumstances, wondering what is happening and how long until the "appointing" will take place. During these in-between times, we run out of answers and are stripped of all our securities. God teaches us that His ways are higher than ours and that His plans and timing are best, even when we don't fully understand them. David knew that he had been *anointed* to be king, and yet he had not been *appointed* yet. His heart had to learn to beat in unison with God's heart, and that lesson was to be learned in the caves and strongholds of the wilderness.

Jesus, the descendant of David and the Savior of the world, also went through an "in-between" time in Gethsemane and on the cross. He asked God if there was any other way than the path He was facing (Matthew 26:39), but there was none, so He submitted to the plan. On the cross, feeling separated from His Father, Jesus uttered the words from Psalm 22, a psalm of David: "*My* God, *My* God, why have You forsaken me?" (Psalm 22:1; emphasis added. Also see Matthew 27:45). Jesus usually called God His Father, but this time He called Him His God! That's all He had left! His God! And even though He was feeling forsaken, He still used the possessive pronoun: *My*. Why was He forsaken, being that He was "Immanuel, God with us" (Matthew 1:23)? He was forsaken so that we may never be forsaken. And this is why I am assured of my salvation. Nothing can separate me from God's love through Jesus! Nothing! (Romans 8:38, 39).

During his time of persecution and suffering David found *permanence*, *protection*, and *faithfulness* in the Lord. God became his rock, his refuge, and strength. Are you "in-between"? Are you feeling persecuted, abandoned, treated unfairly, or alone? Remember, you are not alone! God is with you, at your side. He will strengthen you and guide you. He will uphold you and sustain you. He is the One who anoints and the One who appoints. In the meantime, let Him teach you to pray and sing from the heart—after God's own heart.

Individual or Small Group Study Questions

1. Why are in-between periods (the time from leaving point A and before reaching point B) necessary for growing our faith? What is the purpose of the "wilderness of the soul"?
2. Do you believe that God wants the best for us, as soon as possible? Why or why not?
3. Share a visualization of God that you need right now: "Lord, You are my _____"
4. What does it mean to have intimacy with God during the good and not so good times?
5. What is the significance of Jesus quoting Psalm 22 as He was hanging on the cross?

CHAPTER 5

Exhausted

The postal employee must have thought I was crazy as I frantically knocked on the glass door of the central post office distribution center after hours. There was no way that person could have known the reason for my desperation and exhaustion.

It had started eight years earlier when I enrolled in the doctoral program at a university in the United Kingdom with a renowned New Testament scholar as my dissertation supervisor. During the previous eight years I had periodically traveled from the United States to the United Kingdom to work on my degree, but now the time was running out. I still had some final touches to make in order to finish my dissertation, and the deadline was approaching fast. My supervisor had just returned my dissertation draft with his notes, and I was planning to take it with me to Alaska, where I was scheduled to be preaching and teaching the following week. My plan was to use every spare moment I could find to finalize the dissertation and then send it to the binder and distribute the finished product to the members of my defense committee. This was my last chance to finish the degree; there was no more time left. Somehow I missed the delivery and ended up with a note on my door saying that the package was at the postal distribution center. I called the number on the note and was told that the office would be closing in a few minutes. I tried frantically to explain how important it was for me to get the package that day and how eight years of hard work and thousands of dollars were on the line. Someone took pity on me and said that an employee would stay there a little longer after the office closed, but that I had to hurry and be there within twenty minutes. I drove like a maniac with the weight of eight years on my shoulders; however, I could not make it within the time I was given. Exhausted, I arrived at the post office, but it looked totally deserted. I started knocking, but no one answered. I felt drained and desperate as tears started filling my eyes. Yet I kept knocking and knocking, hoping against all hope.

This was it. Since I couldn't get my manuscript with the professor's remarks, I wasn't going to make it. This was my only chance because I was flying out in a few hours. But it couldn't end here—it just couldn't! I kept knocking, because there was nothing else I could do. Finally, after what seemed like an eternity, somebody came to the door and gave me the package. I could not stop thanking him, but he will probably never know how much his kindness meant to me. And I will never forget that day, on which my academic future hung in the balance. It would have ended right there if it wasn't for the grace of God and the kindness of that person. I will also never forget feeling totally spent and the helplessness that brought tears to my eyes. But that wouldn't be the last time in my life I felt that way.

A time to cry

What else could possibly go wrong? I am sure that David asked this question repeatedly, and each time he found out that, actually, something else did go wrong. This is a sad time in the life of the anointed of the Lord. Having spent a long time living in caves and strongholds, exhausted from wandering, David finally decides to seek refuge in the enemy camp—in Gath, of all places (1 Samuel 27:1–7)! What? Isn't this the hometown of Goliath? Yep! This is the territory of Israel's enemies, and David has decided to cross over to the other side. What happened to the triumphant youth who trusted in the Lord of hosts? The life in caves, the cold of the night, the thirst of a sun-scorched land, and the hopelessness of a desperate soul can sometimes have this effect on a person. And yet God doesn't abandon us, even when we make wild decisions and take crazy detours. He is right there, by our side, waiting patiently for us to come to our senses. David spends sixteen months

God doesn't abandon us, even when we make wild decisions and take crazy detours.

in Gath and is given a small town, Ziklag, as a home for himself and for his men and their families. *No psalm is recorded from that period of time.* Sad, isn't it? In the darkness of the soul it's easy to lose one's hope and one's song. And as if living in the enemy territory isn't bad enough, David turns double-faced. The king of Gath is led to believe that David has turned to his side, but David can't harm Israel and makes raids against desert tribes instead, killing everyone so no one can report what he is doing (see verses 8–12). He lies and covers it up with bloodshed. This is a sad time in the life of David.

But one day it goes from bad to worse. The Philistines are about to go to war with Israel. What is David to do? The king of Gath invites David and his men to join them in the battle (1 Samuel 29:3). But the commanders of the Philistines are suspicious and angry; they still remember how *this* David was the one who led Israel to victory; "Is this not David, of whom they sing in the dances, saying. 'Saul has slain his thousands, and David his ten thousands'? " (verse 5). So the king sends David and his men home. Thus, God miraculously delivers David from a lose-lose situation. But when they arrive at Ziklag, there is a nightmare awaiting them! "The Amalekites had made a raid on the Negev and on Ziklag, and had overthrown Ziklag and burned it with fire; and they took captive the women and all who were in it, both small and great, without killing anyone, and carried them off and went their way" (1 Samuel 30:1, 2). What else could have gone wrong? *Everything!* Talk about being enrolled in the school of brokenness! Not only is David's double life in a total mess in the enemy territory, but now their town is burned down and, more importantly, their families have been kidnapped!

Exhausted and drained, these tough, battle-hardened warriors in desperation started to cry. "When David and his men came to the city, behold, it was burned with fire, and their wives and their sons and their daughters had been taken captive. Then David and the people who were with him lifted their voices and *wept until there was no strength in them to weep*" (verses 3, 4; emphasis added). Yes, the time of crying had come. Exhausted, David is about to hit the bottom; but the amazing thing is that when we lose everything and all that's left is God, we discover that *God is enough* . . .

Look up!

In this most disheartening of circumstances, David finds out that there are no guarantees in life, other than God's love and His Presence with us. He could have used a bit of encouragement and comfort from his people, but they were not happy with him. "David was greatly distressed because *the people spoke of stoning him*, for all the people were embittered, each one because of his sons and his daughters" (verse 6; emphasis added). Have you ever encountered someone who will kick you when you are down? If so, you can relate to David. Everything is going wrong, but until now, at least he had his "friends," even though they were a bunch of discontented misfits. But now, even his people have turned against him, and they are about to stone him!

David has hit the bottom! And the amazing thing about the bottom is that we get a chance to look up. And that's exactly what David did. The verse we just read ends with this amazing statement: "*But* David strengthened himself in the LORD his God" (verse 6; emphasis added). Woo-hoo! I love the pivotal "buts" of Scripture, and this is one of them. *But*—regardless of what was happening—David still had *his God*! And he still trusted that his God would strengthen him and answer him. And he didn't leave it there. He remembered that God was with him! He talked with Abiathar the priest, who had been with David since crazy king Saul had massacred all the priests at Nob for talking with David (see 1 Samuel 22:14–23). The priest had the ephod, which contained the Urim and Thumim to communicate with God. In this manner David asked the Lord, "Shall I pursue this band? Shall I overtake them?" (1 Samuel 30:8).

And God said, "Go, David! Go!" and David, having

Regardless of what was happening—David still had his God!

cried his eyes out, pursued the enemy because God had said to, and he trusted *his God*! I love that David still

> *God's GPS is able to recalculate and reroute your path, no matter how deep you may have gone into the "enemy camp."*

believed that God was with him and would be faithful to His promise. Believe that God wants to communicate with you, too, even when you have hit the bottom. People who have taken detours sometimes believe that God doesn't want them anymore. If you are there today, remember that you will find God the very moment you seek Him; you will find God because He never left! And He has plans for you, like He had plans for Israel (see Jeremiah 29:11–13). God's GPS (grace positioning system) is able to recalculate and reroute your path, no matter how deep you may have gone into the "enemy camp."

Exhausted yet blessed . . .

David and his men came to a brook named Besor: "So David went, he and the six hundred men who were with him, and came to the brook Besor, where those left behind remained. But David pursued, he and four hundred men, for *two hundred who were too exhausted to cross the brook Besor remained behind*" (1 Samuel 30:9, 10; emphasis added). What? How can anybody be so *exhausted* that they give up the search for their families? I have never been to the Brook Besor, but I understand that it has steep banks, and these men were just too exhausted to go on. Sound familiar?

You can read the story of the amazing victory that God gave David and his men in verses 11–20. They recovered all the wives, children, spoil, and other things that had been stolen (verses 19–20). What a triumphant victory for the man after God's heart! What a joyful day for the one who had been hiding and in distress! It was time to celebrate! When David and the four hundred men came back to the Brook Besor, the other two hundred exhausted men who were waiting came out to meet David and he greeted them (verse 21). "Then all the wicked and worthless men among those who went with David said, 'Because they did not go with us, we will not give them any of the spoil that we have recovered, except to every man his wife and his children, that they may lead them away and depart' " (verse 22). Can you believe it? They thought it was *their victory*! And they didn't want to share it!

And this is where you see David's heart: "Then David said, 'You must not do so, my brothers, *with what the* LORD *has given us*, who has kept us and delivered into our hand the band that came against us. . . . For as his share is who goes down to the battle, so shall his share be who stays by the baggage; they shall share alike.' So it has been from that day forward" (verses 23–25; emphasis added). David recognized that none of them were *entitled* to anything and that the Lord had given them what they had! So, they shared. And the exhausted men were as blessed as those who went into the battle! I absolutely love it! Why, you ask? Because this is a core principle of the gospel. Let me explain.

None of us *deserve* salvation, no matter what we have or have not done. Jesus died for us and, in doing so, won the victory for all who choose Him. And He shares the results of His victory with all of us, who are too handicapped and exhausted to be able to run the perfect race that would qualify us for eternal life:

> *He will divide the booty* with the strong;
> Because He poured out Himself to death,
> And was numbered with the transgressors;
> Yet He himself bore the sin of many,
> And interceded for the transgressors (Isaiah 53:12;
>   emphasis added).

The "strong" in this context are the ones who believe in what He has done. This is *truly* the best news ever! We are all winners, because Jesus *wins*!

So, if today you find yourself tired, exhausted, and with tears in your eyes, remember that Jesus has already won the victory on your behalf. Accept His tender and compassionate invitation: "Come to Me, all who are weary and heavy-laden, and I will give you rest. Take my yoke upon you . . . and YOU WILL FIND REST FOR YOUR SOULS" (Matthew 11:28, 29).[1] Go ahead: Breathe! Relax! Rest! You are blessed!

Individual or Small Group Study Questions

1. Recall a time in your life when, just like in David's life, things went from bad to worse and you found encouragement in the Lord, your God.
2. Is there ever a "time to cry" for the children of God? Why or why not?
3. What did you learn from the Brook Besor event in the life of David?
4. What is the theological importance of the fact that the exhausted ones, who had been left behind, shared in the same spoils as those who had fought the enemy?
5. Has Jesus truly won the victory for us? If so, why are we so often still anxious?

---

1. For additional reading on Matthew 11:28–30, refer to my book *I Will Give You Rest* (Nampa, ID: Pacific Press®, 2015).

CHAPTER 6

Nurtured

I had driven a long way to get there and arrived the day before the meetings were scheduled to start. I was the main speaker at a large weeklong gathering in Arizona, where I had to speak every day. I do this often, sometimes several times a month, but this time felt different. When I arrived, I felt rather weak. I thought that with a good night's rest I should be back to normal. However, during the night I started feeling even worse. Due to my asthma, any congestion in my lungs can turn into something serious, but I was hoping that this was not the case because my assignment was very important. Furthermore, I had similar meetings scheduled for the following week in Washington State.

The time for the first evening meeting came, and I could barely stand. I remember lying down on a sofa behind the platform right before speaking. I asked God to help me get through this meeting without fainting and then to give me some guidance as to what to do next. God blessed me with supernatural strength during my talk. Afterward, as I was resting in my room, I became convinced that I had to leave and take care of myself.

Nurtured

Still, it was a very hard decision; in order to get home I had to drive for many, many hours. Thankfully, my parents lived closer, only some seven hours from the meeting venue. Immediate arrangements were made for a replacement speaker for this venue as well as the meetings in Washington, and I decided to try to make it to my parents' house. I asked God to give me miraculous strength so that I could drive to my parents' home where the best care and medical attention were readily available. To this day, I remember the long grueling drive and how I felt when I finally got to my parents' place. I had arrived at a peaceful haven where I could rest and be nurtured. I felt extremely weak and had to make a great effort to get there. The doctor confirmed that my condition was very serious and prescribed medication and rest for at least two weeks. My parents were happy to take care of me until I regained my strength. Several days later I started to take short walks in the backyard in order to get some sun and fresh air. I was feeling so thankful for their love and care, I knew I was wanted and welcome there, I could stay as long as I needed. They comforted me in a thousand ways. When I recite the words of Psalm 23—"He takes me to green pastures and waters of rest, and restores my soul" (verses 2, 3, author's paraphrase), images of my loving parents, who nurtured me and provided everything I needed physically, emotionally and spiritually, still come to mind. Are you in need of provision and rest? Nurture and restoration? Read on! God is an expert in rest and relaxation (R & R) for the soul.

The Lord is *my* Shepherd

For us, Psalm 23 will serve as an interlude between two major seasons in David's experience: his early life and his years as a fugitive (1 Samuel) and the years of his kingship (2 Samuel). As I mentioned earlier, this remarkable psalm became even more special for me when my dad recited it right before he passed away. I based my homily for his memorial service on this psalm of assurance and comfort, and in the process I gained some insights that will stay with me forever.

Yahweh Roi, the Lord my Shepherd, is a very special name that David assigns to God. In the ancient Near East in general, and in Israel in particular, *shepherd* was a common metaphor for a king or a religious authority figure. David, the shepherd-king, is now implicitly placing himself as a sheep in the care of the heavenly Shepherd-King. Because he uses the first person possessive pronoun, Yahweh is not only *the* Shepherd of His people, but *my* Shepherd, the One who comforts and nurtures me. When we place ourselves under this heavenly Shepherd-King, we will

> *W*hen we place ourselves under this heavenly Shepherd-King, He will provide for our needs.

not live in a constant state of neediness because He will provide for our needs.

The flock finding food, rest, and comfort in green pastures and restful waters helps us visualize the abundance of provision. The Greek Old Testament (LXX) uses the same word here for "waters of *rest*" as the one found in Jesus' invitation in Matthew 11:28–30: "Come, and I will give you *rest*."[1] God wants His sheep to know they have a Shepherd and that they can trust in Him! No need to live in worry! The Shepherd provides for our physical as well as our spiritual and emotional needs: "He restores my soul; He guides me in the paths of righteousness for *His name's sake*" (Psalm 23:3; emphasis added). It is His name, His honor that is on the line, because He is in charge of His sheep!

Over the years, I have collected some information about sheep because they are a commonly used scriptural metaphor for describing the people of God in need of His guidance.[2] In doing so, I have learned that in general sheep are very helpless animals. They can't find food or water by themselves; they need constant protection from predators; they would easily drown if they tried to drink in deep water; and they can't rest if there are problems, like tension in the flock or bugs that bother them. Sheep are absolutely and completely dependent on the shepherd to provide everything for them, including a peaceful and quiet place, green pasture, restful waters, and everything else. The sheep don't know where they are or where they are going; they just need to follow their shepherd (sounds just like us, doesn't it?).

David, himself a shepherd, proclaims that the Lord is *his* shepherd, and his own survival depends on the presence of his Shepherd.

You are with *me*!

Many books have been written on Psalm 23; every phrase is meaningful, and I wish we had space to analyze each word in detail. One of the most outstanding features of this psalm is the fact that the first part (verses 1–3) is narrated in the third person singular, talking *about* the Lord and what He does: He is my shepherd; He makes me lie down; He leads me; He restores my soul; He guides me. But then suddenly everything changes. When the psalmist enters the dark valley of the shadow of death (verse 4), he unexpectedly switches to the second person singular and begins talking in a prayer *with* God: "I fear no evil for *You are with me*" (verse 4; emphasis added). This is the center and the core of the psalm: *You are with me*!

My dad was a minister, and he talked *about* and *with* Jesus for more than forty years. And when he walked through the valley of death, he trusted *his* Shepherd to guide him, nurture him, and ultimately save him for eternity. It was striking to me that my father faced death with absolutely no fear! There is something about pain, suffering, darkness, and death that makes God absolutely real and personal to each one of us. When facing death, He is all we have, and we find out that He is more than enough! The presence of the Shepherd is the only antidote for fear: "I fear no evil, for You are with me."

Then David continues as a guest of his Shepherd-King. He is treated in a manner fit for a guest of honor: "You prepare a table . . . ; You have anointed my head with oil; my cup overflows" (verse 5). According to the customs of the ancient Near East, you were welcome to stay as long as the host kept your cup full. As soon as your cup started drying out, it meant that it was time to go. David's cup

We find out that He is more than enough!

is overflowing—the King is welcoming him with open arms! He can stay! That's the way I felt in my parents' place: their care for me was abundant and overflowing! I love this picture of David being lavished by God's grace! Yes, dear one, you are loved in the same way! Bask in the grace of God!

The writer of the psalm knows that he is highly favored by God! And I love the next verse: "Surely goodness and lovingkindness will follow me all the days of my life" (verse 6). The verb in Hebrew is literally "pursue"—God's goodness and grace pursue us, follow us! God is passionately in love with us! What an incredible picture of God! And David visualizes himself dwelling in the presence of Yahweh, *his Shepherd*, permanently, without end. "I will dwell in the house of the LORD forever" (verse 6). Even though the Hebrew text could suggest the meaning "throughout the years," I believe that David was talking about eternal life: being with God forever, beyond this earthly life. And we too can be assured of eternal life, because *Jesus wins*! And He is *our* Shepherd!

The Good Shepherd

The Scriptures frequently refer to the Savior using the Shepherd-King metaphor. In the Old Testament the prophecy of the coming prince, a descendant of David, is clearly pointing to the Messiah who would come to shepherd God's people. For example, Ezekiel 34 is a prophecy against the shepherds of Israel who have let the sheep get lost and go hungry (please read the whole chapter to get a glimpse of how God feels about us, His sheep!). After denouncing the shepherds for their carelessness, God promises the forthcoming Shepherd-King: "Then I will set over them one shepherd, My servant David, and he will feed them; he will feed them himself and be their shepherd" (Ezekiel 34:23). This prophecy was written many years after David's death, and it refers to a coming descendant of David.

Your Shepherd intimately knows you, and He has laid down His life for you.

Nurtured

When Jesus, the awaited Davidic king, came to live and die for us, He identified Himself with the metaphor of the Good Shepherd. "I am the good shepherd; the good shepherd lays down His life for the sheep. . . . I am the good shepherd, and I know My own and My own know Me, even as the Father knows Me and I know the Father; and I lay down My life for the sheep" (John 10:11, 14, 15). Yes, my dear friend, Jesus *knows* everything about you, and He will take care of you. Your Shepherd intimately knows you, and He has laid down His life for you. That's how much He loves you!

And the visualization continues all the way throughout the Bible, to the very end and into eternity. In the book of Revelation, in an amazing blend of metaphors, Jesus, who is the Lamb, becomes the eternal Shepherd of His people: the Lamb is also the Shepherd! "The Lamb in the center of the throne will be their *shepherd*, and will *guide* them to springs of the water of life; and God will wipe every tear from their eyes" (Revelation 7:17; emphasis added).

I don't know what you are going through in your life, but God does. Perhaps you are tired—needing nurturing and restoration—your Shepherd offers that. Or maybe you, like David, have been mistreated, persecuted, and oppressed, and you need a safe place to rest; your heavenly Shepherd prepared that for you. Or maybe you are facing the end of your life, walking through the valley of the shadow of death, and need to be assured of eternal life through the merits of Jesus accounted on your behalf; your Shepherd guarantees that! You can *rest assured*! So, fill in the blank with your name, and personalize God's promise for you, one of His beloved sheep:

"The Lamb in the center of the throne will be _____'s shepherd; and will guide _____ to springs of the water of life; and God will wipe every tear from _____'s eyes" (Revelation 7:17, author's paraphrase).

Individual or Small Group Study Questions

1. How do we reconcile Psalm 22:1 with Psalm 23:1?
2. Explain the meaning of this verse: "He guides me in paths of righteousness for His name's sake" (Psalm 23:3).
3. How exactly does God restore our soul by taking us to green pastures and waters of rest?
4. What is the significance of David switching from the third person (talking about God) to the second person (talking to God) in verse 4 of this beloved Psalm?
5. Jesus spoke of Himself as the "Good Shepherd" (John 10). How does this picture of Jesus make a difference in your life?

---

1. For an in-depth study of this theme, see my book *I Will Give You Rest*.
2. This paragraph is quoted from Talbot, *I Will Give You Rest*, 78.

$\mathscr{F}$ulfilled

We met in a public place, not far from my house. Her eyes betrayed lack of sleep and a weary spirit. Susan[1] was hitting bottom and needed help. Barely looking up, she told me her story about the dark pit she found herself in, from which she couldn't get out. She had started working for a ministry, but her boss was constantly putting her down and hindering her growth in many ways. This affected her so severely that she started in an emotional downward spiral and now found herself at the very bottom of the pit of addiction, alone, desperate, feeling totally helpless and hopeless.

I learned that she had several advanced degrees and soon realized that I was dealing with a very intelligent person with a keen mind and a wealth of knowledge. Yet at this time, she was in total darkness and couldn't even imagine any light at the end of the tunnel. We arranged for subsequent meetings, and I gave her quite a bit of reading and homework to do before our next meeting. As time went by, she started trusting, little by little, that God had something better for her and that she would be given the strength she needed. Gradually her face started to light up and she could smile again. Even though she was still at the same job, she knew it was only a matter of time.

Several months later she was offered a position as a full-time university professor. She had her doctorate and now was given the opportunity to put it to good use. She was beside herself! I was wondering how this time of "abundance" would affect her after a time of darkness. And I saw the miracle with my own eyes: her strength and confidence were renewed, her spirit was exuberant—and her faith in God fully restored. She became a bright arrow, pointing her students to a graceful God. I still see her sometimes, and every time I praise God for her flamboyant demeanor. She used to be in a dark pit, *nevertheless* God took her out of there and placed her feet on a solid rock! Have you ever wondered what happens after the cave, the desert, the pit, the darkness?

> *She became a bright arrow, pointing her students to a graceful God.*

I waited patiently for the LORD;
And He inclined to me and heard my cry.
He brought me up out of the pit of destruction, out
   of the miry clay,
And He set my feet upon a rock making my footsteps
   firm.
He put a new song in my mouth, a song of praise to
   our God;

Many will see and fear
And will trust in the LORD (Psalm 40:1–3).

What comes after the dark night of the soul is a big woo-hoo!

Hold on to your hat!

The second book of Samuel starts with the news that Saul and his son Jonathan have died. David mourns, chanting a heartfelt lament recorded in 2 Samuel 1:19–27. I can understand why he would mourn for his friend Jonathan, but only a man after God's heart could mourn the death of the crazy king who had made his life so miserable. After the dirge we find David asking God if he should go to a city in Judah, and God answers that he should go to Hebron (2 Samuel 2:1). "Then the men of Judah came and there anointed David king over the house of Judah" (verse 4). Finally! After all these years of strongholds and caves, it's finally happening! Waiting after his anointing for a painfully long time until his appointing, he's finally there! Now he is king of Judah, the southern kingdom, while Ish-bosheth, the son of Saul, is made king of the northern kingdom of Israel (see verses 8, 9).

But God, didn't You anoint me king over all *of Israel?*— David could have asked. But God doesn't do things our way or according to our timing. David will become king over all of Israel three chapters later (2 Samuel

5:1–5), and right from the beginning of the narrative we are told how long he reigned: "David was thirty years old when he became king, and he reigned forty years. At Hebron he reigned over Judah seven years and six months, and in Jerusalem he reigned thirty-three years over all Israel and Judah" (verses 4, 5). Yes! God does fulfill His promises!

The next two verses are very meaningful to me. "Now the king and his men went to Jerusalem against the Jebusites, the inhabitants of the land, and they said to David, 'You shall not come in here, but the blind and lame will turn you away'; thinking, 'David cannot enter here.' *Nevertheless*, David captured the stronghold of Zion, that is the city of David" (verses 6, 7; emphasis added). Did you catch that? You *cannot*, you *will not*, there is *no way . . . nevertheless* he did! I absolutely love it! I was first introduced to this "nevertheless" notion through Max Lucado's book *Facing Your Giants*,[2] which I recommend for an insightful read on the life of David. Lucado points out that we all, like David, can have a *nevertheless* written in our biographies when we allow God to act. This area that David conquered to make his royal dwelling had not been defeated by Israel, so far (see Joshua 15:63; Judges 1:21; 19:10–13), and its inhabitants were quite confident that David could not do it either! (see 2 Samuel 5:6). *Nevertheless*, he did! And this place became David's Jerusalem.

I definitely have a *nevertheless* bio. And when I read

the Bible, I find that all the chosen characters have *nevertheless* bios as well. Remember Elijah, who became depressed and suicidal; Moses, who committed murder and was eighty years old when God spoke to him; Sarah, who was barren and past childbearing age; Paul, who persecuted Christians. *Never-*

> *The* only reason for David's *nevertheless* was Yahweh's presence in his life!

theless Elijah ascended to heaven without tasting death; Moses delivered Israel from Egypt; Sarah bore the son of the promise through whom the Israelites came; and Paul became the apostle of grace! And you? Yes, you! You have a *nevertheless* in your bio too!

And "David became greater and greater, for the LORD *God of hosts* was with him" (verse 10, emphasis added). The only reason for David's *nevertheless* was Yahweh's presence in his life! The same holds true for us. Yes, when God says, "It's time," hold on to your hat! A flamboyant season has come!

Uncensored worship

When my husband, Patrick, and I got married, we were both coming out of a difficult relational past. We both had definitely traversed deserts of the soul. And when we met each other, we felt blessed by God, and a new hope was born in our hearts. We chose a biblical text for our wedding that is still very meaningful to me, even though seventeen years have passed since we got married. These verses represent the darkness of the winter passing and the spring arriving: "The winter is past, the rains are over and gone; flowers appear on the earth; the season of singing has come" (Song of Songs 2:11, 12, NIV). I believe that this is what was happening to David in the next episode; this same exuberant reality: the time of running and hiding was past, and the season of singing had come!

After years of hiding in deserts and caves, now he was the king of Israel, dwelling in his own royal city. And David, being a man after God's heart, wanted God's presence at the center of his kingdom and decided to bring the ark of the Lord to Jerusalem. "And David arose and went with all the people who were with him to Baale-judah, to bring up from there the ark of God which is called by the Name, the very name of the LORD of hosts who is enthroned above the cherubim" (2 Samuel 6:2). Unfortunately, in his euphoric happiness, David forgot the Lord's instructions on how to transport the ark (see Exodus 25:12–14; Numbers 4:5, 6, 15; 1 Chronicles 15:13–15) and instead placed the ark on a cart pulled by animals, as the Philistines had done (see 1 Samuel 6:7). This important oversight ended up in a tragedy (you can read about it in 2 Samuel 6:1–11), and David felt angry and fearful, abandoning for a time his plans to bring the ark to Jerusalem (verses 10, 11).

But when David realized that the ark had brought

blessings to the home where it was left, he decided to try again. This time the Levites carried the ark of the covenant, according to God's instructions (1 Chronicles 15:25, 26). When the bearers had gone six paces, David made a sacrifice to the Lord. And at one point his heart erupted in praise and thanksgiving! His joy became exuberant because the time to praise and worship had come! It was time to sing, play instruments, and make a joyful noise! "And David was dancing before the LORD with all his might, and David was wearing a linen ephod. So David and all the house of Israel were bringing up the ark of the LORD with shouting and the sound of the trumpet" (2 Samuel 6:14, 15). What a woo-hoo moment! I imagine that heaven will be like this, with the expression of flamboyant joy for our salvation and eternal redemption. Woo-hoo!

But as is often the case, someone didn't approve of such exuberant display of praise and worship. In the midst of this flamboyant scene Michal, David's wife and daughter of Saul, "looked out the window and saw King David leaping and dancing before the LORD; and she despised him in her heart" (verse 16). David was not wearing his royal robe but only a linen ephod (verses 14, 20), and his wife, Michal, felt embarrassed and judged him. How often I

He has done marvelous acts on our behalf and is worthy of our praise!

have seen this same critical spirit in places of worship. So many people confuse personal preferences with biblical principles and judge those who worship differently! We need to realize that there may be great variety in the way people worship because of cultural and generational differences. The principle given by Jesus Himself is to worship Him in spirit and truth (see John 4:23), and yet many will try to impose their own way of worshiping upon others. When Michal sarcastically criticized him, David tried to explain that he didn't do this for others but for the Lord (see 2 Samuel 6:21, 22) and reminded her that God had chosen him over her father as king of Israel. The episode ends with a sad note: "Michal the daughter of Saul had no child to the day of her death" (verse 23), indicating that what she did was displeasing to God. Sometimes we will have to learn to ignore the voices of those who criticize our way of relating to God if we are to fulfill His plans for us. Don't let anyone take away the joy of your salvation! Be flamboyant, be exuberant, just like we will worship in heaven! (See Revelation 4; 5; 14:1–5; 15:2–4, etc.). He has done marvelous acts on our behalf and is worthy of our praise!

Nevertheless redemption

I will be eternally grateful for my fulfilling life after the "cave" experiences. If you find yourself in a dark place today, may you find hope in this chapter. Our gracious

Fulfilled

God takes us out of darkness into His marvelous light! All of the redemption history, the whole Bible, is a *nevertheless* story. Humanity rebelled against God (Genesis 3), *nevertheless* God intervened and sent Jesus to die on our behalf.

Abraham lied, Joseph got desperate, Moses killed someone, David dwelled in caves and eventually sinned greatly, John the Baptist doubted, Paul persecuted Christians, and so on; *nevertheless*, God didn't give up on us. Instead He sent a Savior through the lineage of Abraham, preserved a remnant through Joseph, and delivered His people through Moses. David became their king in the promised land, and a thousand years later John the Baptist announced that the descendant of David was coming as the awaited Messiah to establish the kingdom of heaven forever, and Paul became the herald of the good news!

Because of Jesus, all of us are offered a *nevertheless* biography! Let's accept it and live in constant flamboyant celebration of our *nevertheless* redemption that our Creator and Redeemer offers freely to every one of us! Woo-hoo!

Individual or Small Group Study Questions

1. What exactly is the *new song* that God puts in our mouths when He brings us out of the pit? (see Psalm 40:1–3).
2. God's timing is not ours. Do you trust Him when His timing doesn't match yours?
3. Explain the relevance of having a *nevertheless* biography.
4. Having spent years hiding in caves David had become king. What made his wife uncomfortable about his exuberant worship of the Lord? Do we still struggle with the same attitude?
5. Read Romans 8:28. Have you experienced God's ability to bring good from *everything* in your life? How is it possible?

---

1. Name and identifying facts have been changed to preserve anonymity.
2. Max Lucado, *Facing Your Giants* (Nashville: Thomas Nelson, 2006).

CHAPTER 8

*A*ppointed

Memories flooded my mind as I walked into the church where my father's memorial service was about to take place. Eleven years earlier another significant event—my commissioning service—had taken place in the same church. It is a service in which my denomination officially and publicly recognizes that God has called the particular person to ministry. In my case, it happened after I had spent five years in full-time ministry, the last two of which I had served as the senior pastor of the church in which I was about to give the homily in celebration of my dad's life.

Eleven years earlier it was my dad who had stood behind the same pulpit to give the homily for my commissioning service. He had spoken about Jesus, the Good Shepherd, and what it meant to be called to shepherd God's people. I remembered his words with deep emotion: he had felt that after more than forty years of ministry he was "passing the torch" on to me. It is hard for me to describe my feelings as I recalled his spoken words. A few years before I had gone through a very difficult time, as one dream after another got shattered right in front of me. Yet somehow God had made all things work together for good and, after all these challenges, called me to ministry. And there I was, asking the same questions that David had asked in response to the covenant God had made with him: "Who am I, O Lord GOD, and what is my house, that You have brought me this far?" (2 Samuel 7:18). Now, eleven years later, my father was resting in the Lord. Yet the fact that Jesus is our Good Shepherd (John 10) and gave His life for His sheep, thus securing eternal life for us, was my comfort, my hope, my assurance, and the theme of my homily for his memorial service.

I have discovered in my life that God chooses and appoints for a special calling those who are *the least and the last* so that all the glory may be given to Him who calls, not to those who are called. This was true even when He chose Israel, the least of the nations, and David, the youngest of his brothers, to be the king of Israel. God doesn't call us because of who we are; He calls us because of who He is. In the words of the famous song by Casting Crowns: "Not because of who I am, but because of what You've done; not because of what I've done, but because of who You are." In this chapter we will rejoice in the understanding that God is in control of our lives,

God sees what we can't see, and He has plans that we can't even imagine.

as well as our calling and the timing of our *appointment*, and that He guides us "in paths of righteousness, *for His name's sake*" (Psalm 23:3; emphasis added).

God's covenant

When David had finally settled in his royal house and could rest from his enemies (2 Samuel 7:1), he felt that it was not right for the ark of the Lord to be in a tent while he was living in luxury (verse 2). And the Lord answers his concern in a very interesting way. It goes something like this: "You want to build a house for me? It is I who will build a royal house for *you*!" (read verses 4–16). And God goes on to enumerate His intervention in David's past, present, and future. I absolutely *love* this section of Scripture! God reminds David that everything good in his life has happened because of His providence and that David would be part of the covenant of redemption. If you look carefully, you will see how often the first person pronoun is used by God in His response (verses 8–16): *I took you* from being a shepherd to being a ruler; *I have been* with you; *I have cut off* your enemies. In other words, *All of it is My work! And I am not done yet*—says God—*I will make you a great name, I will appoint a place of rest for My people, I will make a house for you, and I will establish your descendant* (who, by the way, will build a house for Me). How about you? Do you ever struggle with what to do next? If so, take a moment to draw a time line of how God has guided your life in the past, marking off important milestones in your life. You will be amazed at how He has orchestrated your life, too, and you will find it safe to entrust your future to Him as well. Your past, present, and future are secure in God's hands. I believe that if we want to fulfill God's purpose for our lives, we need to be enrolled in the school of brokenness for one main reason: we need to learn to give up control and abandon our agendas regarding what our lives are supposed to look like. God sees what we can't see, and He has plans that we can't even imagine. The school of brokenness teaches us to let go and let God.

> The school of brokenness teaches us to let go and let God.

God's covenant with David is very important because it is part of His overall covenant with the human race in the redemption history. The whole Bible is one big covenant in which God reveals His plan to redeem humanity. The most important Bible characters in the covenantal story are Adam, Noah, Abraham, Moses, David, and Jesus. Obviously there are many others, but these biblical figures receive or offer additional signs and understanding of God's covenant with the human race. And in this narrative (2 Samuel 7:4–16), the Lord reveals to David how the covenant will continue—even beyond David's time: "When your days are complete and you lie down with your fathers, I will raise up your descendant after you, who will come forth from you, and I will establish his kingdom. He shall build a house for My name, and I will establish the throne of his kingdom forever. I will be a father to him and he will be a son to Me" (verses 12–14).

God doesn't treat us according to what our iniquities deserve; He treats us according to the covenant He has made through the blood of Jesus, our Redeemer. How amazing is that? Wow! "See what great love the Father has lavished on us, that we should be called children of God! And that is what we are!" (1 John 3:1, NIV). We are children of the King! And how do you respond to such an amazing covenantal revelation and faithfulness?

A prayer after God's heart

"Who am I?" (2 Samuel 7:18). Yes! That's the only possible response! "Who am I, O Lord GOD, and what is my house, that *You have brought me this far*? And yet this was insignificant in *Your* eyes, O Lord GOD, for *You* have spoken also of the house of *Your* servant concerning the distant future. . . . For the sake of *Your* word, and according to *Your* own heart, *You* have done all this greatness to let *Your* servant know. For this reason *You* are great, O Lord GOD, for there is none like *You*, and there is no God besides *You*" (verses 18–22; emphasis added). *You, Your, You, Your, Your, Your, You . . . ALL You, Lord!* Broken people know in their heart of hearts that they are unworthy of the grace that is bestowed upon them. A man after God's own heart will never feel entitled to be saved or to any position of honor. We are the surprised and amazed children of God, who throughout eternity will continue to ask the same question: Who are we that God would treat us as royalty? We are the unworthy children of the King, ordinary people who have accepted the extraordinary grace of the King of kings.

> *B*roken people know in their heart of hearts that they are unworthy of the grace that is bestowed upon them.

As you probably read on the cover of this book, there are twelve videos that accompany these twelve chapters. The video for this chapter includes a song, written and performed by our very own Jesus 101 production director, Chris James. The words of the song depict exactly how David felt, and how we all feel, when faced with the outrageous grace of God:

What can one give the Giver of life,
What can I offer the One who has all
Well, I feel so small and You are so tall,
And I'm overwhelmed by it all.

Chorus
Unworthy, unworthy that's me,

Appointed

Unworthy I'll always be,
Unworthy of the grace that You give,
Yes, I'll always be the unworthy one.

Well, I try so hard but I always fall short,
I give You my all but it's never enough,
Well, I feel so small when You are so tall,
And I'm overwhelmed by it all.

Now if I should start to feel proud of myself,
And worthy of being the son of a King,
Remind me of what you did up on that cross,
And humble me Lord once again.

"Forever" kingdom

Both the Lord and David refer to the "forever" characteristic of God's covenantal kingdom (see verses 13, 16, 24, 25, 29). God unveiled to David the future by revealing to him that his descendants would establish a *forever* kingdom: "Your house and your kingdom shall endure before Me forever; your throne shall be established forever" (verse 16). Obviously, God's promise went beyond David's son, Solomon, all the way to the Davidic Messiah, the One who was to come to deliver God's people and break the yoke of their oppression (see Ezekiel 34:23–31). When we get to the New Testament narratives, everyone is talking about a *kingdom* that is coming, ruled by a Davidic king. Several times the Gospel writers add details to remind us that Jesus is the much-awaited Davidic king (for example, see Matthew 1:1; Luke 1:32). On many occasions, Jesus is called "Son of David," especially in the Gospel of Matthew, which was written mainly for a Jewish audience.

When we accept Jesus as our Savior and King, we become citizens of that forever kingdom. I still remember, many years ago, how I became a citizen of the United States. It was a memorable and emotional event filled with joy as thousands of us celebrated, singing and waving the United States flag. I can't even imagine what it will be like when we finally arrive at the royal palace of the heavenly kingdom! All I know is that through Jesus Christ I am already a citizen of the kingdom of God, and this reality permeates every day of my life. When I lost my parents, I knew I would see them again because they are citizens of the heavenly kingdom as well. This eternal kingdom is given to us as a gift through the death and resurrection of Jesus. Not long ago, when we reopened my parents' tomb to bury my dad, I placed a large key in it. You see, Jesus is coming again, and He promised to raise the citizens of His kingdom to eternal life. Jesus said: "I have the keys of death" (Revelation 1:18; compare with 1 Thessalonians 4:16), and I fully trust His covenant with us. When Jesus returns as the "KING OF KINGS, AND LORD OF LORDS" (Revelation 19:16) and comes to wake up my parents to enter His forever kingdom, He will find this symbolic key I placed there in full assurance of His faithfulness.

I don't know what I will do when I get to heaven: jump, sing, hug Jesus, be silent, praise and worship—I can't even imagine. But one thing I know: I will take off my crown and place it at the feet of the *only One worthy* of praise: the forever Davidic King, my Redeemer, Jesus!

Individual or Small Group Study Questions

1. Why is it important to acknowledge that God guides you in every step of your life?
2. How does God's Covenant affect you personally?
3. Do you ever feel unworthy of God's favor and salvation? Is that healthy or not?
4. Is it possible for us to have the assurance of being citizens of God's "forever" kingdom?
5. How do you respond to God's unmerited grace?

CHAPTER 9

$\mathcal{V}$indicated

It was a very long, yet fruitful and joyful, day. I was in Ohio leading a series of meetings in a convention center, where we were studying the Gospel of Luke, using my book *Luke: Salvation for All*[1] as a study guide. This book contains many stories that point to the undeserved and totally outrageous grace of God. In one of the chapters, I tell the story of a girl wearing glasses who had changed my life when I felt very much like an outsider. When I was twelve years old, my family moved from Argentina to Michigan because my father was sent to study, for his master's degree, at Andrews University. Lynell was a very compassionate girl, she took me in and became my best friend during the year we spent there. I always remembered her kindness even though I had never seen her again. Now, almost forty years later, I was in Ohio. After the meetings that day, as I was conversing with some of the attendees who had stayed to talk with me, I noticed a family waiting for me: a man, a woman, and a young lady in her early teens. They waited patiently until almost everybody else had gone and then came to me. There was a moment of silence as we looked at each other until the husband spoke up, pointing to his wife: "This is the girl with glasses!" he said.

Quite shocked, I looked at the woman standing in front of me. "Lynell?" I whispered in disbelief. Tears filled her eyes and mine. We embraced and cried—and embraced and cried. There was a small group of people around us who were totally clueless as to what was going on. When I finally was able to catch my breath, I started to explain with great emotion that this was the girl with glasses who had treated me so kindly when I was twelve years old. Everyone got so excited about it that they wanted to take photos and videos of us. I still keep several photos and videos on my iPhone to remind myself of the occasion.

Lynell, however, kept saying: "But I didn't do anything." I tried to explain to her how she had changed my life by opening up her heart to me. She had given me clothes and other necessities that we did not have, she had shared her life with me! We would play together and study together, her family would take me to a concert, and much more. And most importantly she gave me a new identity that I desperately needed; I was loved and accepted in this new country, and that was priceless. Yet she kept saying, "I didn't do anything; you were my friend." And naturally that

A person after God's heart never keeps score of their good deeds.

is what friends do, and they don't keep score because a person after God's heart never keeps score of their good deeds. It's natural for them. Thank you, Lynell!

The story that we will experience in this chapter is one of those stories of friendship and love that reminds us of God's heart, filled with love, compassion, and undeserved grace.

The promise

When David was running for his life, God provided a loving and supportive friend for him: King Saul's son, Jonathan. It was an unlikely friendship, because Jonathan would have been the natural successor to his father, yet he knew that David had been chosen by God to be king of Israel. Instead of feeling jealous or suspicious, Jonathan loved David, and they became best friends. "The soul of Jonathan was knit to the soul of David, and Jonathan loved him as himself" (1 Samuel 18:1). As the narrative continues, Jonathan becomes increasingly aware of the certainty that David will be taking over the kingdom (see 1 Samuel 18:1–4; 20:12–17; 23:17). In spite of that understanding, his love for David creates a deep bond that results in a covenant between the two: "Then Jonathan made a covenant with David because he loved him as himself. Jonathan stripped himself of the robe that was on him and gave it to David, with his armor, including his sword and his bow and his belt" (1 Samuel 18:3, 4). Even though this incident is narrated at the beginning of their relationship, the specifics of the covenant are not revealed until later (1 Samuel 20:13–16). Many believe that this gesture of transferring the royal attire to David was a sign of Jonathan's abdication of the throne or at least that he was surrendering to whatever God's will might be in the matter.

Later on, when it becomes obvious that David must run for his life and enroll in the school of brokenness, Jonathan seems certain that one day David will be king and asks him to keep his descendants safe when he does. "You shall not cut off your lovingkindness from my house forever, not even when the LORD cuts off every one of the enemies of David from the face of the earth. So Jonathan made a covenant with the house of David. . . . Jonathan made David vow again because of his love for him, because he loved him as he loved his own life" (verses 15–17). And so this covenant, this promise is secured between these two unlikely friends.

This promise is secured between these two unlikely friends.

But how would this vow be carried out? I am so glad you asked!

Whom are you looking for?

If we fast-forward David's life through his time in the cave, the school of brokenness, and several years later, we come to the time when he is king over all of Israel, just as Jonathan had predicted. And this is where we find the most amazing narrative in 2 Samuel 9: "Then David said, 'Is there yet anyone left of the house of Saul, *that I may show him kindness for Jonathan's sake?*' " (verse 1; emphasis added). This question of David must have been quite shocking, given the customs of the time. Whenever a new dynasty came to power, the first order of things was to make sure that there were no rivals to the throne by exterminating each and every competitor from the previous dynasty (see examples in 2 Kings 10:1–11; 11:1). David, instead, wanted to show *kindness* to Saul's descendants to honor his covenant with Jonathan. The phrase *show kindness* or *show consideration* is repeated three times in this story (2 Samuel 9:1, 3, 7), highlighting that David was being loyal to the covenant with Jonathan.

> *But God sees the heart, and I am so thankful for that!*

A servant of the house of Saul, named Ziba, was brought to David. Ziba informed him of a living descendant of Jonathan: "There is still a son of Jonathan who is crippled in both feet" (verse 3). The son of Jonathan was Mephibosheth, but Ziba does not mention his name—only his handicap. It is sad when instead of their name and character people are identified by their sickness, problem, or sin. Maybe you can relate to that, feeling those judging glances of people. But God sees the heart, and I am so thankful for that!

The son of Jonathan had become crippled when he was a young child: "Now Jonathan, Saul's son, had a son crippled in his feet. He was five years old when the report [of the death] of Saul and Jonathan came from Jezreel, and his nurse took him up and fled. And it happened that in her hurry to flee, he fell and became lame. And his name was Mephibosheth" (2 Samuel 4:4). Many years had gone by since that time; he was an adult now and even had a young son of his own (see 2 Samuel 9:12).

When David inquired about the whereabouts of Mephibosheth, it turned out that he lived with a benefactor in the town of Lo-debar (verse 4), on the other side of Jordan. *Lo-debar* means "desolate" or "without pasture." We can understand why this poor crippled man was living as far as possible from the new king. I love to envision the utter shock of the inhabitants of that desolate town the day David sent for Mephibosheth! Can you imagine a royal caravan coming to this place, in the middle of nowhere, asking for a forgotten lame man? I just love it, love it, love it! This is the perfect picture of God, chasing after us! What a comforting view of God! No matter how far we have gone, His mercy and fanatical love follow us! (see Psalm 23:6).

You will do *what*?

Very few stories in David's life reveal his heart like this story. These are the moments when you see how the school of brokenness changes the human heart to seek after God. When Mephibosheth came to the king, he must have been trembling, because the first words out of

David's mouth, after calling him by name, are "Do not fear" (verse 7). *Why not? You are the new king, and I belong to the previous dynasty. What do you mean, "do not fear"!* "Do not fear, for I will surely show kindness to you for the sake of your father Jonathan, and will restore to you all the land of your grandfather Saul; and you shall eat at my table regularly" (verse 7). *Excuse me! I don't think I heard you right . . . you will do what? Show kindness to me? Why? Restore to me my grandfather's land? Why? Invite me to dine regularly at the royal table? What is going on?*

"Again he prostrated himself and said, 'What is your servant, that you should regard a dead dog like me?' " (verse 8).

> *God's grace is bestowed upon the utterly unworthy.*

This self-deprecating title always caught my attention: "a dead dog like me." It's almost palpable how, unable to understand such unmerited favor from the king, he felt that way about himself. But this is God's way: His grace is bestowed upon the utterly unworthy. David was vindicated as a covenant keeper, even though he had been accused by Saul of trying to usurp the throne and had been hunted down by the same dynasty that he now honored. He was a man after God's own heart! And Jonathan was vindicated as a close and cherished friend of king David, who honored their covenant. And Mephibosheth was vindicated and treated as royalty, because he was the recipient of this covenant of grace. We truly see the image of God in covenant-keeping people and true friendships bonded with God's surprising love.

Everything happened as David said. Jonathan's son, crippled in both feet (verse 13), moved to Jerusalem and ate regularly at the royal table: "Mephibosheth ate at David's table *as one of the king's sons*" (verse 11; emphasis added). As one of the king's sons! Wow!

The King's table

The truth is that in many ways I am crippled myself, emotionally and spiritually. I don't deserve salvation. I am a sinner in a desolate and sinful land. Nevertheless, I have been adopted as one of the King's children, and you have, too. Jesus left heaven and came to this sinful world, keeping His covenant as the Creator-Redeemer. He refused to go through eternity without us, and He died so that we could live again with Him and eat at His table forever! Everyone, not just one group, is invited to accept the King's offer.

> *Jesus refused to go through eternity without us, and He died so that we could live again with Him and eat at His table forever!*

Jesus Himself spoke of the scope of this invitation: "I say to you that many will come from east and west, and recline *at the table* with Abraham, Isaac and Jacob in the kingdom of heaven" (Matthew 8:11; emphasis added).

I imagine how Mephibosheth must have felt, eating at the king's table. I imagine him sitting at the table, dangling his crippled feet, filled with surprise and gratitude. And I imagine myself with my crippled heart, sitting at the royal table in the kingdom of heaven, next to you, swinging my feet and exclaiming: "See what great love the Father has lavished on us, that we should be called children of God! And that is what we are!" (1 John 3:1, NIV).

Woo-hoo!

Individual or Small Group Study Questions

1. Have you ever been the recipient of surprising (astonishing, extraordinary, staggering, amazing) grace? Explain.

2. Do you trust God's promises? What difference do they make in your daily life? Share one of your favorite Biblical promises.

3. David was a man after God's own heart. How was God's heart reflected in David at the time when he showed kindness to Mephibosheth?

4. List parallels between the way David treated Mephibosheth and the way God treats us.

5. What does it mean to be a child of the King of Kings?

---

1. Elizabeth Talbot, *Luke: Salvation for All* (Nampa, ID: Pacific Press®, 2011).

Chapter 10

Exposed

Have you ever wondered why we build more rapport with some people rather than with others? It turns out that we feel more connected with successful people who are openly "not perfect" and vulnerable than with those who seem to have it all together and never make mistakes—at least not publicly. Even communication experts explore this *connection phenomenon*. Check out these articles on the topic.

"Showing vulnerability. Psychologists often need to build trust quickly with patients, and may do so by dropping a pen, spilling coffee or telling a bad joke. Research shows that people like best those high-performing people who make a mistake—after they have established their credibility. . . . Sharing vulnerability with your team, such as singing really badly in a karaoke bar, can help you bond and develop trust."[1]

In a classic study led by Elliot Aronson at the University of Texas at Austin in the 1960s, "participants listened to a taped interview of a college student trying out for the College Quiz Bowl team. . . .

". . . In one version, the 'candidate' answered 92% of

the questions correctly and had been an honors student, the yearbook editor, and a member of the track team in high school.

"A second version had this exact same beginning, but tacked onto the end of the interview was a pratfall: The candidate spilled coffee. . . .

". . . Strangely enough, it turned out that they thought most highly of the high-performing person who'd spilled their coffee."[2]

Unlike the stories of the ancient cultures in Egypt and Mesopotamia, where the characters were typically portrayed as superhuman, never-erring heroes, the Bible reveals both the good and the bad sides of its characters. This is a constant pattern in the Bible, even with heroes through whom God had achieved great things. Moreover, this characteristic provides one of the core authentications of the historicity of the Bible. One of the reasons why characters such as Moses, David, and Paul fascinate us, and help us, is that they were not perfect. As a matter of fact, they had great downfalls, such as murder and adultery, and God's grace was sufficient for them. And, therefore, they are like each one of us, and we find application and comfort when we read about their

One of the reasons why characters such as Moses, David, and Paul fascinate us, and help us, is that they were not perfect.

lives. This chapter brings me great assurance because, in this stage of his life, David spilled more than a cup of coffee.

Downfall

God honored king David and called him a man after His own heart (see 1 Samuel 13:14; Acts 13:22). God even used David as the "model" king, as the standard by which all other kings were measured (see 1 Kings 11:4–6; 14:8, 9)—with one exception: "David did what was right in the sight of the LORD . . . *except* in the case of Uriah the Hittite" (1 Kings 15:5; emphasis added). Big exception, don't you think? What happened? Oh, let me tell you . . .

When everyone went to war, for some reason David stayed in Jerusalem (2 Samuel 11:1). "Now when evening came David arose from his bed and walked around on the roof of the king's house, and from the roof he saw a woman bathing; and the woman was very beautiful in appearance. So David sent and inquired about the woman. And one said, 'Is this not Bathsheba, the daughter of Eliam, the wife of Uriah the Hittite?' " (verses 2, 3). The story should have ended there, even for a king. She was married. That's it! End of story! But this time David thought that he was above the divine law. Authority mixed with lust is a bad combination.

Uriah the Hittite was a member of the elite thirty men (see 2 Samuel 23:39). His name means "Yahweh is my light," which may imply that he was actually born in Israel or changed his name at some point. The great Hittite empire had fallen, but some remnants could be found in Syria. Somehow Uriah was now in Israel and, did I tell you? He had a *wife named Bathsheba*! King David sent for her and lay with her (2 Samuel 11:4). And in soap-opera style, the next verse introduces a bombshell: "The woman conceived; and she sent and told David, and said, 'I am pregnant' " (verse 5). "I am pregnant" is one of the most dreaded statements in illicit sexual relationships; it is up there along with comments like "I have a sexually transmitted disease," "I will tell your spouse," or "I have photos to prove it."

So now David comes to his senses, asks for forgiveness, and makes things right, right? Wrong! We enter the second major section of 2 Samuel 11, where we see David bargain with his sin, trying to cover it up at any cost. David recalls Uriah from battle and makes the most macabre efforts to entice him to go lie with his wife, so that everyone might think that the child is his (there was no DNA testing back then). You can read this incredibly evil orchestration in verses 6–13. But Uriah was more noble than David had expected, and the plan backfired: "Uriah said to David, 'The ark and Israel

So now David comes to his senses, asks for forgiveness, and makes things right, right? Wrong!

and Judah are staying in temporary shelters, and my lord Joab and the servants of my lord are camping in the open field. Shall I then go to my house to eat and to drink and to lie with my wife? By your life and the life of your soul, I will not do this thing.' " (verse 11). Sexual abstinence was expected of soldiers on active duty (for examples see 1 Samuel 21:5; Deuteronomy 23:10). Uriah is honoring his king and his God; but David is doing neither.

So *now* David comes to his senses, asks for forgiveness, and makes things right, right? Wrong! He goes to the next stage. Because he is not just having a fall; he is diving into a downward spiral. He is not just spilling his coffee; he is swimming in the mud. And of all things, he starts plotting murder! David sends orders to Joab to place Uriah in the fiercest battle that he may die, and Uriah is *so* loyal that he carries in his hand his own death warrant (2 Samuel 11:14, 15). As planned, Uriah is killed in battle, and after a few days, "David sent and brought her [Bathsheba] to his house and she became his wife; then she bore him a son" (verse 27). Well . . . maybe David got away with it. Maybe they came up with the perfect explanation: now they were married, and they had a baby, and, yes, he was a couple of months premature, but who was going to argue with the king, right? Not so fast. The chapter ends with an ominous sentence: "But the thing that David had done was evil in the sight of the LORD" (verse 27).

You are the man!

Time goes by, but David has not acknowledged his sin. So the Lord initiates the intervention through Nathan, the prophet, who will tell a parable to David. This is a judicial parable that elicits a judgment. (For other examples of spoken or acted parables of judgment see Isaiah 5:1–7; 1 Kings 20:35–43; 2 Samuel 14:1–20.) The story is about a rich man who owns many flocks and herds in contrast to a poor man who has only one little ewe lamb that is like a daughter to him. When the rich man receives a traveler, he acts very hospitably, but behind the scenes his evil deeds condemn him. Instead of taking from his own flock and herds, he takes the only ewe lamb of the poor man and prepares it for his guest (read 2 Samuel 12:1–4). Hearing the story, David was outraged! And as it was his custom to pass judgment in legal matters, he is absolutely sure that this man deserves to die and that a fourfold restitution must be made (verses 5, 6). David is beside himself because of not only the treacherous act itself but the wretched character of the man who completely lacks any moral boundaries and has no compassion at all.

Then comes the application—Nathan turns to David with "*You are the man!*" (verse 7), and explains how God has been so generous with him (verses 7, 8), while in this instance David has despised the Lord! "Why have you despised the word of the LORD by doing evil in His sight? You have struck down Uriah the Hittite with the sword, have taken his wife to be your wife, and have killed him with the sword of the sons of Ammon" (verse 9). Wow! And just like that, suddenly David was completely exposed. How would you like to walk into a place one day and find someone openly speaking about all the skeletons in your closet? What a shock! David thought he was above it, but God knew every detail of what he had done. God knows *everything*! Every shameful thought and secret desire. Nathan goes on to explicitly enumerate some of the consequences of David's sin, one of which is that this child will not survive. What a sad, sad day for the shepherd-king, and what a contrast with those days when he used to delight in singing songs to his God with a restful soul and peaceful heart! They are now a distant echo as his heart is broken by his own sin.

Finally, having attempted to cover it up, David now confesses his sin: "Then David said to Nathan, 'I have sinned against the LORD.' And Nathan said to David, 'The LORD also has taken away your sin; you shall not die' " (verse 13). There would be terrible consequences to his sin, yet God would spare the life of David. It is amazing and encouraging how David, having confessed his sin, immediately

> *I*t is amazing and encouraging how David, having confessed his sin, immediately rediscovered his poetic voice and started writing psalms again.

rediscovered his poetic voice and started writing psalms again. Psalm 51 is one of the most beautiful psalms of repentance, which he wrote at this time. But, now that David had fallen and had attempted to cover up his sin and then, after God's intervention, had also repented, would God still bless him and keep His covenant with the Davidic dynasty? I love your question! It is a very important question, the answer to which is vital for every one of us.

The Sin Bearer

This is incredible! Are you sitting down? You probably have heard about the wisest man who has ever lived on this earth: King Solomon. Under his reign, God fulfilled the prophetic promise of the geographical scope of Israel's territory promised to Abraham back in Genesis 15:18. Well, do you know who his parents were? Check this out: "Then David comforted his wife Bathsheba, and went in to her and lay with her; and she gave birth to a son, and he named him Solomon. Now *the LORD loved him*" (2 Samuel 12:24; emphasis added). What do you mean? God blessed David and Bathsheba with the wisest man on earth? What point

Jesus Christ is the Sin Bearer, and He not only carried our sins and transgressions but also purchased the right to bless us, heal us, and give us peace!

was He making? Why would He bless them like that? Oh, my friend, Jesus Christ is the *Sin Bearer*, and He not only carried our sins and transgressions but also purchased the right to bless us, heal us, and give us peace! How outrageous is that! "He was wounded for our transgressions, He was bruised for our iniquities; the chastisement for our *peace* was upon Him, and by His stripes we are *healed*" (Isaiah 53:5, NKJV; emphasis added). And the crazy thing is that Bathsheba made it into Jesus' genealogy, because Jesus came from the David-Solomon lineage (see Matthew 1:6).

The school of brokenness teaches us to see ourselves in the true light. David learned that there is a big difference between *covering* up his sins and his sins being *covered*. Jesus has made ample provision to assure us that our sins will be *covered* with His blood, and we are utterly blessed when we let Him do so:

David also speaks of the blessing on the man to whom God credits righteousness apart from works:

"BLESSED ARE THOSE WHOSE LAWLESS DEEDS HAVE
   BEEN FORGIVEN,
AND WHOSE SINS HAVE BEEN COVERED.
"BLESSED IS THE MAN WHOSE SIN THE LORD WILL
   NOT TAKE INTO ACCOUNT" (Romans 4:6–8).

Paul quoted these verses from an amazing psalm of David, Psalm 32:1, 2; here the apostle explains that the righteousness that saves us is not ours—but Christ's. So, if you are wondering what happens after a great fall, let me tell you that I know how the story ends. You and I might have to live with the consequences of our sins on this earth, but we won't have to live wondering if we can be at peace with God or if our sin has been forgiven or if we can be saved. Jesus has covered us! "Therefore there is now no condemnation for those who are in Christ Jesus" (Romans 8:1). I want to make sure you got it, so fill in the blank with your name: "Therefore there is now no condemnation for _____, who is in Christ Jesus" (Romans 8:1, author's paraphrase). Got it? Woo-hoo!

Individual or Small Group Study Questions

1. David had committed many sins throughout his life. Why did God single out the sin against Uriah and not any other? (1 Kings 15:5).
2. What is the emotional and spiritual dynamic of a down-spiral, like the one David experienced in his life?
3. God initiates interventions and sends Nathans to us. How does it affect your daily life?
4. Explain the difference between us covering up our own sins, and our sins being covered by God (read Romans 4:6–8).
5. Read Romans 8:1. How does this apply to David? How does it apply to you?

---

1. "How to Win Your Team's Trust With Better Communication," Quick Base (blog), January 18, 2017, http://www.quickbase.com/blog/how-to -win-your-teams-trust-with-better-communication.

2. Adam Galinsky and Maurice Schweitzer, "The Secret to Getting Other People to Trust You Quickly," *Fast Company*, December 8, 2015, https:// www.fastcompany.com/3054275/the-secret-to-getting-other-people-to -trust-you-quickly.

Chapter 11

Challenged

Many years ago some people whom I was really close to had hurt me deeply. It was a very difficult and pivotal time that changed a lot of things in my life. I was trying to decide what to do next and was exploring several options. While I was facing this challenging situation, someone gave me an audio tape on forgiveness. As I listened to it, my soul was profoundly affected.

It was a story of a man and his two pets, a dog and a bird. The three of them had a fun life together, and the dog used to sit by the man, who was his best friend. They enjoyed each other's company very much! One day the man returned home to find the bird missing. He looked everywhere but could not find it. Deeply saddened, he sat in his regular spot, and he noticed some feathers in his dog's mouth. It was obvious that the dog had eaten the bird. The man could not believe that his dog would do such a thing, and a deep separation occurred between the man and his dog. The man decided to keep the feathers close to his chair. For several days the dog didn't come around his master because he could sense that he was deeply displeased with him. After a few days, the dog started coming close to the man's chair, but whenever he got close, the man would rub the feathers on the dog's nose, reminding him of what had happened, which perpetuated the continued separation between the two.

The story went on with more details that I don't remember, but the gist of it was that when we forgive someone, we shouldn't keep reminding them of what they have done, especially those close to us. Forgiveness is not a payment plan or a lifelong vengeance where we make the other person pay in small perpetual payments with interest for what they have done. On the other hand, forgiveness is not a denial or condoning of the wrong that was done; and it is not a lack of appropriate boundaries. Yet even when we need to detach for obvious reasons, we can learn to detach with love and not hate. The story was a call to self-evaluation regarding the feathers that we keep lying around, which we might use whenever we feel like it to remind the other person of their offense. I was deeply touched and eventually preached a sermon entitled "Feathers," and it was based on the life of David.

God fully paid the debt Himself at the cross because of His love for us.

When we have been through the school of brokenness, we learn that no one will ever owe us as much as we owe God, who fully paid the debt Himself at the cross because of His love for us. In this chapter we will study an event in which David was betrayed and challenged by someone very close to him. And even though he was the king, David responded very differently than Saul did when he felt threatened by David's youthful popularity. After all, David was not like Saul because he was a man after God's own heart.

When the unthinkable happens

David's moral fall with Bathsheba had consequences, even within his own family. When the prophet Nathan had presented to him "the case," David demanded a four-fold restitution by the offender (2 Samuel 12:6). Sadly enough, David lost four of his sons in unthinkable circumstances. One of his sons, Absalom, had a beautiful sister named Tamar; and their half brother, Amnon, also a son of David, was in love with her. The sad story is told in 2 Samuel 13; please take a moment to read it. Amnon sexually violated Tamar, committing incest and ruining her life. "Now when King David heard of all these matters, he was very angry" (verse 21). Angry? That's it? That's all we get? That's all Tamar gets? The king was angry? It seems that David's own embarrassing past was preventing him from taking charge of the situation. Two years passed in silence (verse 23); that deafening silence should have been broken by the voice of truth—but it was never heard.

Challenged

By the way, if you ever witness an injustice, speak up! Your voice matters! You are the voice for those who have lost theirs!

Absalom got tired of waiting and took vengeance into his own hands (which is not a wise idea, no matter how sad the situation) and devised a plan to kill Amnon (verses 23–29). Having succeeded, Absalom fled to his grandfather's house in Geshur and remained there for three years (see verses 37, 38). David's heart was devastated; he had lost both of his eldest sons, one to death and the other to exile (verse 39). After Joab arranged an interesting enacted parable (2 Samuel 14:1–21), Absalom was permitted to return to Jerusalem, yet he was not allowed to see the king's face for two more years. By now it has already been seven years since the wrong done to Tamar. Seven years! Isn't it amazing how things that are not resolved or brought to justice linger forever? After a "fiery" dialogue with Joab (see verses 28–33), Absalom finally was able to see his dad, "and the king kissed Absalom" (verse 33). Even rough-looking and seemingly hardened young men long for their parents' love and approval! Don't ever miss the opportunity to share love and encouragement

Don't ever miss the opportunity to share love and encouragement with your kids, even when they have disappointed you.

with your kids, even when they have disappointed you. So, now we are all good, right? Not so! We are just getting started . . .

Progression

Nothing happens in a vacuum. Absalom's progression down his path is sobering, and it reminds us of the danger of an unchecked heart. His sister was terribly violated, and he had the right to expect justice for her. He took her in to live with him, which was a compassionate *response*, even though he was wrong to suggest she should stay silent (2 Samuel 13:20), obviously thinking it to be the best course of action in that culture. Yet when nothing was done about her, he *reacted* by taking justice into his own hands and killing the perpetrator (verses 28, 29). He goes into exile for three years; and seven years after the event Absalom *rebels* against his father by starting a conspiracy to take over the kingdom. At first, it wasn't an overt rebellion: he merely presented himself in a very royal manner and acted as if he had all the answers to the administrative problems of the kingdom (2 Samuel 15:1, 2). But eventually he declared himself king in Hebron (verses 10–12), the place of his birth. Then he entered Jerusalem and decided to prove his authority by publicly humiliating his father, taking David's concubines for himself "in the sight of all Israel" (2 Samuel 16:22). The story has a very sad ending: Absalom died in the confrontation between both armies. "Now Absalom happened to meet the servants of David. For Absalom was riding on his mule, and the mule went under the thick branches of a great oak. And his head caught fast in the oak, so he was left hanging between heaven and earth, while the mule that was under him kept going" (2 Samuel 18:9). When Joab heard about it, he and his men killed him (verses 14, 15). What a dreadful progression of rebellion, and what a terribly sad ending.

On the other hand, David also experienced a progression just the opposite way. Having been trained in the school of brokenness, the old king knew his own sin and shortcomings. He cried a lot and didn't seek vengeance. On the contrary, he kept pleading for the life of his son to those in charge of his army. Some have argued that David was weak because of his past problems. But even though his family was greatly affected by the lack of moral leadership on his part, as I study this situation I see a humble and surrendered heart. When David hears that Absalom is proclaiming himself king, in humility and tears he leaves Jerusalem, passing over the Kidron brook toward the wilderness (see 2 Samuel 15:13–23). When the Levites followed him

David submits to whatever God's will is, knowing that he won't lose the kingdom unless God has decided so.

with the ark of the covenant, for the presence of God to be publicly with David, "the king said to Zadok, 'Return the ark of God to the city. If I find favor in the sight of the LORD, then He will bring me back again and show me both it and His habitation. But if He should say thus, "I have no delight in you," behold, here I am, let Him do to me as seems good to Him' " (verses 25, 26). In the midst of this betrayal and conspiracy, instead of defending himself, David submits to whatever God's will is, knowing that he won't lose the kingdom unless God has decided so. Weeping, he ascended to the Mount of Olives (verse 30). He endured curses that were hurled at him (2 Samuel 16:5–14) and all kinds of humiliation. Finally, when it became clear that the two armies would meet, he pleaded for his betrayer, his dear son: "The king charged Joab and Abishai and Ittai, saying, 'Deal gently for my sake with the young man Absalom.' And all the people heard when the king charged all the commanders concerning Absalom" (2 Samuel 18:5).

What kind of heart is this, that loves even when betrayed and challenged? Oh, I am so glad you asked! It is a heart after God's own heart. I am so touched by David's response to the news of Absalom's death: "The king was deeply moved and went up to the chamber over the gate and wept. And thus he said as he walked, 'O my son Absalom, my son, my son Absalom! Would I had died instead of you, O Absalom, my son, my son!' " (verse 33).

Challenged

But Absalom betrayed him! Absalom conspired against him! Absalom rebelled again his father, the king, and humiliated him in a hundred ways! Oh, you are right. But, "where sin increased, grace abounded all the more" (Romans 5:20). A fanatical love—that's the heart of God.

The King who died

As Gene Edwards emphasizes in his book,[1] David was king, but not after the order of Saul. God used Saul to kill the Saul in David so that when David became king, he wouldn't be like Saul. Many years earlier, Saul, feeling threatened by the talented youth who had been anointed as the future king, pursued him, making several unsuccessful attempts to kill him. David, on the other hand, responded completely differently when his own kingdom was challenged by a powerful and talented youth from his own family. He wept, fled, and humbled himself. He submitted to God's will and loved beyond reason. Who was the "stronger" king? Saul or David? From God's viewpoint, it was the

Jesus, God made flesh, left His kingdom to die in our place that we may live with Him eternally.

shepherd-king who had learned that God's "power is perfected in weakness" (2 Corinthians 12:9). Other divinely chosen leaders, like the apostle Paul, also learned this important truth. God is not looking for a spear-throwing king. He seeks leaders who are willing to enroll in the school of brokenness so that they may respond with a heart like God's.

After all, when the children of God rebelled against Him, the cries of the King of kings reverberated throughout the universe: "O my children, my children, my children! Would that I would die *instead* of you, O my children, my children!" (author's paraphrase of 2 Samuel 18:33). And Jesus was willing to leave His kingdom and come to die a *substitutionary death in the place of* His children. Jesus, God made flesh, left His kingdom to die in our place that we may live with Him eternally, as His royal heirs. I keep putting my name in that verse. I can't help it! Would you like to do the same? Place your name in the blank: "O my child _____, my dear child _____, would that I died *instead* of you, my child _____, my child _____" (author's paraphrase of 2 Samuel 18:33). Yes! The King died for us, His rebellious children, who betrayed Him terribly. And that is the Redemption story!

Challenged

Individual or Small Group Study Questions

1. Explain what forgiveness is, and what it is not (if available, watch video no. 11 of the series, entitled "Challenged").
2. Amnon did not face the consequences of his rape crime until he was killed by Tamar's brother, Absalom. What should have been David's response to the crime in the first place?
3. How did David's actions differ from Saul's when his kingdom was threatened?
4. Why was David so quick to leave the kingdom, allowing God to decide his future?
5. What makes a parent want to die in the place of their child? Why did God choose to die for us?

---

1. Gene Edwards, *A Tale of Three Kings*.

CHAPTER 12

Forgiven

Pride and self-reliance ensured my downfall that day. I still remember it clearly—we were on vacation, camping on the beautiful beaches of Uruguay, my parents' country of birth. I was in the initial stages of learning to drive. My Dad was testing my new skills whenever it was safe to do so. In South America most cars have a stick shift, so there were a few additional things to get used to in order to drive: the coordination between the clutch and the accelerator, the right moment to shift, and so on. We were camped in a small town called La Paloma (the dove), right next to the ocean. That afternoon I asked my dad if I could take the car for a short drive around the campground while he and mom were enjoying a short nap. He agreed.

The car was parked down the hill, not too far from our tent. When I got to the car, I noticed a few kids my age observing me from the top of the hill. I was pretty sure none of them drove and they probably didn't even have access to a car to learn to drive. So I felt very proud and self-confident as I got into the car. I was *so* ready to show off! I decided that this was a perfect opportunity to demonstrate my driving skills to the watching kids, and therefore, instead of backing up slowly, like my dad had taught me, I really stepped on the accelerator. My plan was to pick up some speed in reverse and then suddenly, with a quick twist of the steering wheel, turn the car around and drive away, leaving the onlooking kids in the dust, amazed at my skills. I turned the ignition key, shifted into reverse, and stepped on the accelerator pedal. Then I tried to make a sharp turn to the left. Following my brave maneuver there was one of the loudest noises I'd ever heard: *baaammm!* Completely shocked, I tried to understand what had just happened. Then it dawned on me: I don't know how in the world I had not seen the huge tree! It was humongous, and I had smashed right into it! When I got out of the car, I realized that the front passenger door was literally hugging the trunk of the tree. I was in *big* trouble! I don't remember the expressions on the faces of my "audience" because I didn't want to look at them. Completely ashamed I headed to my parents' tent, looking for words to explain my prideful foolishness.

David went through something similar—but on a much larger scale! He wasn't just driving a car; he was the king of God's kingdom. And somewhere along the line he started to feel pretty good about himself, his authority, his army, and his power. And he faced dire consequences for his self-reliance. Yet even in this darkest of circumstances he learned something amazing that we all need to learn. Read on!

We are looking good!

The following story is narrated in 2 Samuel 24 and 1 Chronicles 21, and we will follow the narrative in the latter. The kingdom has prospered under David's reign, and it is looking good! They are strong and confident. And David starts getting a bit proud of Israel's growth under his care. Even though they were a theocracy, meaning that God was really in charge of the kingdom and that He was the power behind every military victory, David decided that he wanted to know how big and strong his army really was. Whether he wanted to brag about it in front of other nations or simply wanted to rely on the numbers, either way the census wasn't pleasing to God because He knew David's motives behind it! "Then Satan stood up against Israel and moved David to number

Oh, Lord, have mercy on us! Teach us Your ways, and guide our hearts to glorify Your name and not our own.

Israel. So David said to Joab and to the princes of the people, 'Go, number Israel from Beersheba even to Dan, and bring me word that I may know their

number.' . . . God was displeased with this thing." (verses 1–2, 7). The original language reads something like "it was evil in the sight of God." Even Joab, the commander of the army, who was known for his unscrupulous moral behavior, tried to dissuade the king: "Joab said, 'May the

LORD add to His people a hundred times as many as they are! But, my lord the king, are they not all my lord's servants? Why does my lord seek this thing? Why should he be a cause of guilt to Israel?' " (verse 3). Joab realized that David would be guilty if he carried out his plan and that God's disapproval would rest on him. "Nevertheless, the king's word prevailed against Joab" (verse 4). The number of men "who drew the sword" was the focus of the census (verse 5), which indicates that David was interested in knowing the size and strength of his military force. Isn't it something how the human heart is easily enticed by an unhealthy ego pushing for self-trust instead of trust in God?

Consequences and antidote

David realized his evil ways and said to God: "I have sinned greatly, in that I have done this thing. But now, please take away the iniquity of Your servant, for I have done very foolishly" (1 Chronicles 21:8). Believe it or not, it gives me great hope that even a heart after God's own heart sometimes acts foolishly. That way I don't feel alone in my foolishness. When we realize that we have acted against God's will, instead of getting depressed or trying to numb the shame in an unhealthy way, we must come back to God immediately. God answered David through Gad, the seer, offering him a choice of three possible consequences of his sin: three years of famine;

three months under the sword of his enemies; or three days of the sword of the Lord, with a pestilence in the land (verses 11, 12). Hard choices! None of them looked good, and the people would suffer no matter which one David chose. What a humbling thought to realize that those appointed by God to lead are held accountable by God Himself. Oh, Lord, have mercy on us! Teach us Your ways, and guide our hearts to glorify Your name and not our own.

"David said to Gad, 'I am in great distress; please let me fall into the hand of the LORD, for His mercies are very great. But do not let me fall into the hand of man' " (verse 13). I can't imagine that decision! David chose to place himself under God's hand and not under his enemies'. Thousands died from the pestilence, and when the destroying angel was about to enter Jerusalem, the Lord said to the angel: "It is enough; now relax your hand" (verse 15). David pleaded with God to let His hand be against him and his household but to stop the plague over the people (verses 16, 17). In response God gave an *antidote*, a very interesting and specific remedy: "David should go up and build an altar to the LORD on the threshing floor of Ornan the Jebusite" (verse 18). David bought the threshing floor from the Jebusite and erected the altar, and God accepted his

In response God gave an antidote, a very interesting and specific remedy.

sacrifice in a way reminiscent of the prophet Elijah's experience on Mount Carmel in 1 Kings 18: "Then David built an altar to the LORD there and offered burnt offerings and peace offerings. And he called to the LORD and He answered him with fire from heaven on the altar of burnt offering. The LORD commanded the angel, and he put his sword back in its sheath" (1 Chronicles 21:26, 27). And the plague stopped.

It is super amazing that God was able to bring something good even from this terrible situation. Do you remember the verse in Romans 8:28 that reminds us that God will work *all* things together for the good of those who love Him? Well, that always blows my mind, and God managed to do it here as well. Because in the place that David bought, where he offered the sacrifice, not only did he find grace from God, but that was the very spot chosen to build the temple (see 1 Chronicles 21:22–22:1). Can you believe it? This fact is eloquently expressed in the words of Roddy Braun:

> Despite David's guilt in calling for a census of Israel, his sin leads to the designation of the threshing floor of Ornan as the place of Yahweh's choosing for his altar and temple. . . .
>
> That same grace of God which triumphed over David's sins and led to the establishment of God's house remains God's principal attribute available to

human beings. Available through repentance and reaching out to draw and sustain the weak, God himself always takes the lead in lifting up the fallen.[1]

The heavenly *stop* sign

That God is able to reroute our path, no matter how bad our detours, is one of His attributes that I will always be thankful for. All of human history is a giant detour that God was able to redeem by dying in our place. And the most amazing connection emerges from this account after a few years go by: "Then Solomon began to build the house of the LORD in Jerusalem on Mount Moriah, where the LORD had appeared to his father David, at the place that David had prepared on the threshing floor of Ornan the Jebusite" (2 Chronicles 3:1). Did you see that? Oh, this takes my breath away! On the same mountain

> *All of human history is a giant detour that God was able to redeem by dying in our place.*

(Mount Moriah) where hundreds of years before God had stopped Abraham's hand from sacrificing his son Isaac and a substitute animal was provided (see Genesis 22), the same place where David offered the sacrifice and God stopped the angel's hand in the plague (see 1 Chronicles 21 and 2 Samuel 24), on that same mountain the temple of God was built (2 Chronicles 3:1), where the sacrificial system would visually remind everyone that a Substitute was coming in their place. And that was the same mountainous area where Jesus would die.

No hand would stop the sacrifice of God's Son, because He was the *Substitute* that everything else pointed to. *The cross was the heavenly stop sign*, where the penalty for the guilty verdict would be paid. You see, all of us, not just David, deserve death for our sin, yet we have been offered the gift of being set right with God by faith in what Jesus has done for us (Romans 3:23–26). Will you accept the gift? It is eternal life!

I praise God that His grace is greater than all of our detours and sin. And once we accept this grace that cost heaven everything, God offers us a purpose for our lives. He can use us for His glory, in spite of our woundedness! The school of brokenness teaches us to trust that God is in control, that He knows and heals our pain, that He is with us, and that we will live with Him forever. And now, in this very moment, you can accept Jesus as your personal Savior and Lord[2] and choose to live a life of purpose, blessing others and bringing them to our Redeemer to find hope and peace.

> *The* school of brokenness teaches us to trust that God is in control, that He knows and heals our pain, that He is with us, and that we will live with Him forever.

Having a heart after God's own heart is believing that His grace is sufficient—even for us! Join me in praising God for His ability to save! Let's lift up our voices in praise, together, aloud, along with the ancient shepherd-king who had a heart after God's heart:

I waited patiently for the LORD;
   And He inclined to me and heard my cry.
He brought me up out of the pit of destruction, out
   of the miry clay,
And He set my feet upon a rock
   making my footsteps firm.
He put a new song in my mouth, a song of praise to
   our God;

Many, O LORD my GOD, are the
   wonders which You have done,
And Your thoughts toward us;
   There is none to compare with You.
If I would declare and speak of them,
   They would be too numerous to count (Psalm
      40:1–3a, 5).

Woo-hoo!

Individual or Small Group Study Questions

1. David's downfall with the census was caused by pride and self-reliance. Are we typically afflicted with the same faults? How do they affect us?

2. Why did God offer such a distinct antidote to the plague?

3. Talk/write about God's ability to bring good from an entirely bad situation in the case of David buying the threshing floor of the Jebusite (see 2 Chronicles 3:1).

4. How is the cross the heavenly STOP SIGN for the "plague" of sin?

5. Do you accept the gift of the Substitute that Heaven has provided for you? If so, write or share your testimony of accepting Jesus as your personal Savior.

---

1. Roddy Braun, *1 Chronicles*, Word Biblical Commentary, vol. 14 (Word, 1986), 218.

2. If you would like a set of Bible studies to know more about Jesus, please request them at Jesus101.tv. We will be delighted to send it to you free of charge.

For additional FREE resources, videos on demand, daily devotionals, biblical studies, audiobooks, and much more, please visit our website:

www.Jesus101.tv

If you have been blessed by this booklet and would like to help us keep spreading the good news of Jesus Christ through preaching, teaching, and writing, please send your donations to

Jesus 101 Biblical Institute
PO Box 10008
San Bernardino, CA 92423

WATCH the JESUS 101 channel on ROKU!

DOWNLOAD the JESUS 101 app TODAY!